T0152748

# Praise for *Passing Life's Tests:*
## *Spiritual Reflections on the Trial of Abraham, the Binding of Isaac*

"Wouldn't it be great to have a rabbi learned in Jewish texts who also has a sophisticated grasp of cutting-edge contemporary theology? While we are imagining, we might as well give this rabbi an uncanny ability to explain complex ideas in simple ways. And would it be too much to ask for the rabbi to also have a soul—a profound understanding of human beings and a hard-won personal faith? As you read this book, you will marvel at Rabbi Artson's unique combination of gifts. More importantly, Rabbi Artson will accompany you—like a good rabbi should—while you consider the challenging questions arising from Abraham's story, and your own."

—**Rabbi Nancy Fuchs Kreimer, PhD**, associate professor of religious studies; director, Department of Multifaith Studies and Initiatives, Reconstructionist Rabbinical College

"Draws poignantly and pointedly upon Rabbi Artson's own life story as well as upon his vast Jewish and secular knowledge to illuminate and provide original explanations of a text that has been read and debated for millennia. In so doing, he offers the contemporary reader new insights into a controversial and ancient story, and ignites a passion for the wisdom inherent in Torah with his readers. This is an enriching book!"

—**Rabbi David Ellenson**, president, Hebrew Union College–Jewish Institute of Religion

"Rabbi Artson has taken on the most challenging story in the Bible, the binding of Isaac, and has found valuable lessons for all of us in it."

—**Rabbi Harold Kushner**, author, *When Bad Things Happen to Good People*

"Rabbi Artson takes Abraham's test and through personal testimony and deep learning, teaches all of us crucial lessons about faith, learning and love."

—**Rabbi David Wolpe**, Sinai Temple, Los Angeles; author, *Why Faith Matters*

"A book that belongs in every Jewish home. A treasure for all who long to make sense of the Torah's most perplexing narrative. [It] masterfully offers us the tools we need to confront our deepest questions of faith with new eyes and a new understanding. This is a work we will return to over and over again, and with each reading we will emerge transformed."

—**Rabbi Naomi Levy**, author, *Hope Will Find You*; spiritual leader, Nashuva: The Jewish Spiritual Outreach Center

"Through the lens of the Bible's most troubling tale, Rabbi Brad Artson weaves meditations on life's most profound challenges. Life and Bible become intertwined to enrich and enliven one another."

—**Rabbi Dan Ehrenkrantz**, president, Reconstructionist Rabbinical College

"Offers a fresh reading of the text, exhibiting the generosity of spirit and the daring imagination that has always marked the best of Rabbinic Judaism. Artson shows how the text provides an epitome of all that matters to Jewish faith. This is an important read for Christians, both to see a skilled rabbi working with the text and to read of the rich gift that this daringly Jewish text offers to faith. His reading of the text exhibits the deep theological and demanding moral dimensions of Torah faith that goes way beneath conventional religion. In Artson's hands the text arrives at freshness. So will the reader!"

—**Walter Brueggemann**, professor emeritus, Columbia Theological Seminary; author, *The Practice of Prophetic Imagination*

"Invites us to travel the heights and depths of this gripping biblical narrative as a mirror of our own soul's quest. Aided by Rabbi Artson's illuminating translation, multi-layered commentary, and opportunities for deeply personal contemplation, we encounter not only Abraham and Isaac within the story, but our own selves. If you face life-tests that challenge you, use this wisdom well! You will grow in faith, courage and insight!"

—**Rabbi Marcia Prager**, director and dean, ALEPH: Alliance for Jewish Renewal Ordination Program; author, *The Path of Blessing: Experiencing the Energy and Abundance of the Divine*

# Passing *Life's* Tests

## Spiritual Reflections
### on
## The Trial of Abraham, The Binding of Isaac

RABBI BRADLEY SHAVIT ARTSON, DHL

*For People of All Faiths, All Backgrounds*
**JEWISH LIGHTS** Publishing
Woodstock, Vermont

# Also by Rabbi Bradley Shavit Artson

*Love Peace and Pursue Peace:*
*A Jewish Response to War and Nuclear Annihilation*

*It's a Mitzvah! Jewish Living Step-By-Step*

*Making a Difference: Putting Jewish Spirituality into Action,*
*One Mitzvah at a Time*

*The Bedside Torah: Wisdom, Visions, and Dreams*

*Dear Rabbi: Jewish Answers to Life's Questions*

*Gift of Soul, Gift of Wisdom:*
*A Spiritual Resource for Mentoring and Leadership*

*The Everyday Torah: Weekly Reflections and Inspirations*

To the memory of my beloved teacher and *rebbe*,
Rabbi Simon Greenberg, *zekher tzaddik livrakhah.*

To my wife, *eshet hayil*,
Elana,

and to our children, love of our hearts,
Shira and Jacob

*Passing Life's Tests:*
*Spiritual Reflections on the Trial of Abraham, the Binding of Isaac*

2013 Quality Paperback Edition, First Printing
© 2013 by Bradley Shavit Artson

All rights reserved. No part of this book may be reproduced or transmitted in any form or by any means electronic or mechanical, including photocopying, record- ing, or by any information storage and retrieval system, without permission in writing from the publisher.

For information regarding permission to reprint material from this book, please mail or fax your request in writing to Jewish Lights Publishing, Permissions Department, at the address / fax number listed below, or e-mail your request to permissions@jewishlights.com

**Library of Congress Cataloging-in-Publication Data**

Artson, Bradley Shavit.
  Passing life's tests : spiritual reflections on the trial of Abraham, the binding of Isaac / Rabbi Bradley Shavit Artson.
      p. cm.
  Includes bibliographical references.
  ISBN 978-1-58023-631-7
1. Jewish way of life. 2. Isaac (Biblical patriarch)—Sacrifice 3. Abraham (Biblical patriarch) 4. Bible. O.T. Genesis XXII, 1-19—Criticism, interpretation, etc. I. Title.
  BM723.A735 2012
  296.3'11—dc23

                          2012034508

10   9   8   7   6   5   4   3   2   1

Manufactured in the United States of America

Cover and Interior Design: Heather Pelham
Cover Art: © U. Hardberck/fotalia; © mountainpix/shutterstock

*For People of All Faiths, All Backgrounds*
Published by Jewish Lights Publishing
A Division of LongHill Partners, Inc.
Sunset Farm Offices, Route 4, P.O. Box 237
Woodstock, VT 05091
Tel: (802) 457-4000      Fax: (802) 457-4004
www.jewishlights.com

# Contents

# PREFACE
# Why Read This Book?

onsidering God's central role in the Bible and in historical Jewish life, it is well worth considering how we relate to God and how God relates to us. We Jews are often notoriously uncomfortable discussing God. We prefer to leave that to Christians, attributing commandments to the Torah—as if a book could command—and attributing values to the tradition—as though culture were an end in itself. The chasm in Jewish continuity reveals the obvious: books by themselves are not authorities, and traditions are mere repositories unless they transmit significance, holiness, and wisdom. For the sake of Jewish survival, and to make that survival worthwhile, it is time to transcend our discomfort with God and our covenantal memories. It is time to reengage the ancient conversation. And any honest conversation must encompass pain and horror, not simply joy and tranquility. For Jews, that means confronting some biblical tales of terror. Of those tales, the sacrifice of Isaac occupies the deepest depths.

Any Jewish discussion of God and covenant begins, as it must, with revelation—whether and how God reaches out to us. Jewish traditions generally respect God's privacy, choosing to think about God only insofar as God relates to people. What God does when humanity is not looking or involved is God's business, not ours. Neither the Hebrew Bible nor Rabbinic literature offers much insight into God's internal nature, focusing primarily on the Divine-human dialogue.

We will notice that the summons to Abraham erupts with no prior setting of the scene: What was God doing? With whom was God speaking? What motivated God to take this step? On all these points, the Bible maintains the mystery and ineffability surrounding the Divine. God's action is always an eruption, always a revelation. So it is here, with revelation, that we, too, shall begin.

I believe that there is a Holiness that transcends and permeates our world. I believe that this Holiness can best be appreciated by humans in terms of personality—we perceive that this Holiness cares about us and wishes to fashion a partnership with us. Jews call that Holiness "God." Like Abraham, ours is the choice of whether or not to respond. We decide whether or not we say, "*Hineni*—Here I am."

Immediately, however, I must offer two demurrals. Maimonides (Moses ben Maimon, the Rambam), the medieval philosopher and rabbi, correctly points out that language is a human construct, developed to describe human experiences and human emotions. When applied to God, language must necessarily fall short of precise description. Any talk about God is an allusion to something that eludes the limits of language. Any presumption to reduce God to the parameters of human thought or human language is absurd. As the Process philosopher Alfred North Whitehead observed, "The merest hint of dogmatic certainty as to finality of statement is an exhibition of folly" (*Process and Reality*, xiv).

My second demurral flows from the recognition of the limitations we face in talking about God. Because language reflects distinct human perceptions, I also believe that language is specific to particular cultures and particular times. There is no neutral way to transcend our own historical and intellectual context. Consequently, when we talk about God, even recognizing that we must use language metaphorically, we will still reflect the dominant intellectual trends of our own age. Our approach is still embedded in the viewpoint of someone specific from somewhere specific during some particular moment of time.

The same caveat applies for our ancestors. When they describe their experience of Holiness, they naturally use the language of their culture and the images of their time. They, therefore, allude to God as a warrior, a king, or a shepherd. Child sacrifice, patriarchal families, slaves and servants, even animal sacrifice all reflect the culture from which the Bible emerges. In Rabbinic literature, God is additionally described as a rabbi, a teacher, and a sage.

Rather than focusing on these terms in a literal sense, which would undermine their ability to communicate anything at all, we must ask ourselves what aspect of holiness, what cluster of insight, they mean to transmit, to symbolize, to embody just beneath the surface. When the Torah refers to God as "*ish milḥamah*—a man of war" (Exodus 15:3), does it mean to say that God carries a spear, or rather that God is passionate about certain causes, among them freeing oppressed people? When the Torah tells of God demanding the sacrifice of a beloved son as a test, we are invited to derive lessons that swirl and bubble and entice from out of the depths.

I take it to be self-evident that the second path is truer to the genius of the Torah and the intentions of our ancestors. The opening Creation story tells us that God's spirit/wind vibrates over the deep (Genesis 1:2), and it is from the depths that all true creativity emerges.

Language about God is metaphoric, and the Torah's imagery is meant to convey deeper truths about holiness. In what way, then, do we understand the trial of Abraham or the revelation at Mount Sinai? In fact, what do we do with all subsequent Jewish traditions, grounded as they are in words? Do we conclude that they are exclusively the product of human hands and minds, reflecting only their own cultural biases? Are they devoid of any authority or insight for our own age? Does God say nothing to us? No. For the trial of Abraham is true—it accurately confronts us with the ways our core commitments emerge in moments of unrehearsed action. The binding of Isaac is true—accurately elucidating the ways our loyalties can forever scar and mold us. And Sinai is true—it accurately describes, although still as metaphor, the relationship of the Jewish people to that higher reality we recognize as God.

Something happened in the early stages of our people's history that changed their destiny, and ours, forever. At some point, their awareness of God's presence became so overwhelming that they perceived the world in a new and deeper way. In response to an experienced encounter with the Divine, Jews responded by committing their communal identity to that Divine Source. From that time forward, the marriage of the sacred with the ethical, the moral with the ritual, became the central calling of the Jewish people. The Torah represents the attempt of the Jewish people, across millennia, to encapsulate that experience and its implications in stories and laws, in words.

Since the Torah represents the response of the Jews to a heightened experience of God, it is patently impossible and fruitless to argue about whether the Torah is divine or human. It is inseparably both. Just as a flame can only be viewed by an eye, and just as each eye will see the flame in a slightly different way, so, too, the light of God requires active human participation in order to be seen at all. Just as the record of a conversation involves both what is said and what is heard, revelation reflects that mix of divine expression and human perception. Sinai is *matan Torah*, the giving of the Torah, as well as *kabbalat Torah*, the receiving of the Torah. The document itself is the by-product of an interaction that came from both directions.

This understanding of the nature of the Torah carries powerful implications for our own day. In denying that God authored the specific words of the Torah, I do not mean to belittle God. On the contrary, I am asserting that no book, however insightful, can possibly encompass the complete and final will of God for humanity. God's fullness and love are dynamic, always requiring new expression and new commitment.

This fresh translation of Abraham's trial, the binding of Isaac, is an invitation to engage the words of Torah, specifically Genesis 22, and to interpret for ourselves what its imagery continues to convey to us about faith and our relationships today—to ourselves, to each other, to our communities, and to God.

# INTRODUCTION

# Seeing Ourselves in the Biblical Mirror

I n the annals of stories so terrible they rend the human heart, so profound they touch the depths of our souls, and so lofty they reach the highest heavens, none holds pride of place more than the biblical story of Abraham's sacrifice of his beloved son, Isaac. Revered by Jews, Christians, and Muslims alike, contemplated by great secular thinkers as well, this gripping tale shocks us into complete attention, then takes us—in nineteen short verses—on a rollercoaster ride of emotion, challenge, and hope. Known in Hebrew as *Akedat Yitzhak,* the binding of Isaac, it is often referred to in English as the test, or trial, of Abraham. Just who is the tester, who is tested, and what motivates the test all remain open questions that challenge, invite, and provoke us, allowing us to grow in the encounter. The very process of contemplative reading, questioning, and reflection— like life itself—holds the possibility of illumination without resolution. As noted novelist Rebecca Goldstein reminds us, "Answers? Forget answers. The spectacle is all in the questions."[1]

Christians know the story through the book of Genesis and through its affirmation of the centrality of faith in the book of Hebrews (11:17–19), seeing in Isaac's willing sacrifice and Abraham's total faith the foreshadowing of the story of Jesus and the crucifixion. Muslims cherish Abraham's faithful sacrifice of his son—often believed by Muslims to be Ishmael, not Isaac—as told in the Qur'an (37:99–113), honoring the event annually during the Hajj (Pilgrimage) season with the *Eid ul-Adha,* the Festival of Sacrifice.

Jews ritualize the reading of this sacred story, visiting it during the Rosh Ha-Shanah (New Year) services and again during the regular cycle of Torah readings in mid-autumn. Selected as a liturgical reading for one of the holiest days of the year, it is perhaps our inability to come to terms with the incomprehensibility of God's demand, the severity of Abraham's test, the courage of Isaac's willing participation, and the mystery of Sarah's simultaneous presence and absence that makes this narrative impossible to resolve yet impossible to set aside. Secular culture has also produced rich wrestlings with this sacrifice, in poetry such as Wilfred Owen's "Parable of the Old Man and the Young," in literature such as Erich Auerbach's *Odysseus' Scar*, and in visual art through the ages.

In seeking to honor this ancient story, this compact collection of spiritual reflections is offered as a mirror, refracting the light (and heat) of the story and reflecting the contours of a contemporary reading through Jewish eyes. Informed by generations of sages, philosophers, and scholars who have reflected on the *Akedah* in turn, I invite you to use this book as a tool for your own wrestling with the way this powerful tale transcends its own words to force us to confront our own existential sacrifices and our ability to face (and surmount) life's tests.

## Why Study Torah?

The measure of any classic is the degree to which it rewards repeated study. There is surely no collection of writings that can compete with Torah. Across the millennia, Jews, Christians, Muslims, and nonbelievers have been able to glean ever-fresh insights from the Torah and to shed light on life's thorniest challenges through its teachings. Its stories continue to illuminate family relations, love, personal growth, and devotion to life's highest ideals and shimmering temptations.

"Every time a person studies the words of Torah, one finds fresh flavor in them" (Talmud, Eruvin 54b). The laws of the Torah form a yardstick against which social progress may be measured, and a source of healthy criticism against habit, bias, and sloth, an ever-abundant fountain of new meaning and insight.

Perhaps it is for all these reasons that Jewish tradition values Torah study so highly: "Greater is the study of Torah than bringing the daily sacrifice" (Talmud, Eruvin 63b). Another passage in the Talmud goes even further: "The study of Torah is greater than the *mitzvah* of building the *Beit Ha-Mikdash* / Solomon's Temple in Jerusalem" (Megillah 16b).

What an interesting compliment!

The institution of the daily sacrifice itself comes from the Torah. The very requirement to sacrifice in the place that God chooses, in the *Beit Ha-Mikdash,* is found in the Torah. Yet the study of those passages (and of others) is of greater worth than their implementation. Why?

One answer is that "study takes precedence over deed, for study brings about deed" (Talmud, Kiddushin 40b). This is the voice of the realist, of a pragmatic approach to religion. Study is important because it alone can provide guidance for how to implement the lofty principles on which religion stands. Only through regular study can we translate Torah into life, thereby contributing to *tikkun olam*, the repair of the world.

The view of the pragmatist deserves our healthy respect. Too many seekers posit a false dichotomy between action and spirit, as if involvement with the world sullied the soul and distracted from a true inwardness. Valuing learning because it leads to action is an important corrective to this thinly veiled combination of narcissism and callousness: we demonstrate our spiritual vigor to the degree that our spirituality makes the world a more just, compassionate, and healing home for us all.

As important as this practical answer may be, it isn't the end of the search. The tradition also teaches that "those who study Torah, it is as if they had been given the Torah at Sinai" (*Tanhuma, Re'eh*).

Here the purpose of studying Torah (*talmud Torah*) is not to be measured by its consequences. Instead, *talmud Torah* is precious because it allows us to experience nothing less than God's revelation. To encounter God directly isn't a matter of behavior modification, but of opening mind and soul to an encounter with new insight, new contexts, and new priorities. At its core, that is what Torah study is: meeting the sacred and encountering our truest self.

*Talmud Torah* unites the four corners of our lives—intellect, emotions, spirit, and body—into a single outpouring of living. It is at once a pattern of behavior, an insight into being human, a dialogue with the Holy, and a framework of study. We use our learning to fuse Judaism and self into one natural creation, reflecting the sanctity of the Torah in our lives, weaving the threads of our lives into the fabric of our traditions and the Jewish past. We make ourselves anew in God's image, simultaneously adding our own stamp to the sum total of what God's image is.

Another value to Torah learning is its ability to produce community that transcends time and space. In study we join a dialogue that spans the generations, making the youngest Jew contemporary to Abraham and Sarah, to Moses and Miriam, to Hillel and Maimonides. Our voices become instruments in the symphony of Jewish expression, the latest link in a lengthy chain. Through study we gain our own distinct perceptions, refining them in the glow of the ages. And that symphony of learning allows us to join something larger than ourselves, a community that stretches well beyond the fleeting years of our time in this world.

## Finding the Voice of God in Our Texts

When we read and, in this particular case, wrestle with Torah, we open ourselves to a broader vision of our own humanity and a grander context for our own life struggles in the light of great biblical stories. Viewed through the prism of the actions of the biblical patriarchs and matriarchs, we encounter the projection of our own inner struggles and achievements. That countless generations have found resonances to their lives in the echoes of these stories throughout the ages amplifies our own attentiveness and our capacity to encounter our truest selves. This book will illuminate the value of the practice of a contemplative reading of Scripture through sustained attention with one particularly gripping tale—Isaac's sacrifice and Abraham's trial.

As our foundation for this book, I am presenting my own translation of the biblical story, Genesis 22, accompanied by a multilayered commentary. Muslim, Jewish, and Christian traditions all start with an affirmation of divine revelation through sacred Scripture. And they insist, with modern secular readers, on the openness and multivocality of the text made real through active human reading, training our eyes to see beneath the surface, to seek and explore the times the text doesn't flow or fit, the times it tries to distract our focus, the sutures and cover-ups that resist and reward our attention. Engaged reading—religious or secular—is anything but superficial. Consider the fetching imagery of the Zohar, Judaism's mystical classic:

> Woe to the human being who says that Torah presents mere stories and ordinary words!… Torah has a body: the commandments of Torah…. This body is clothed in garments: the stories of this world. Fools of the world look only at that garment, the story of Torah; they know nothing more. They do not look at what is under that garment. Those who know more do not look at the garment but rather at the body under that garment. The wise ones, servants of the Majesty on high, those who stood at Mount Sinai, look only at the soul, root of all, real Torah![2]

The characters, drama, and facts of a biblical story form the framework and structure necessary to proceed, but the recurrent questions and deeper challenges require us to focus on layers of meaning that remain hidden and elusive. The Zohar's words remind us that it is the dynamic, engaged process of reading and interpreting that allows the voice of God to echo just beneath the surface of the text. Without that human depth vision, without training our minds to see beyond the facts, even the biblical text would remain inert. Spiritual, contemplative reading plumbs the depths for added perspective and insight.

A widespread way of presenting the multiple levels of biblical interpretation, borrowing from medieval Christian approaches, asserts that the Torah may be best elucidated along four parallel tracks, whose initial letters, PRDS, form the acronym *pardes*, which, in Hebrew, means "orchard," and is often linguistically (or mystically?) associated with the word *paradise*. This fourfold method is first cited in Jewish sources in the Zohar and later publicized by fourteenth-century Bible scholar Rabbenu Bahya ben Asher, although it was rare indeed that any particular verse was explicated in all four ways or that a commentator was rigorous in using all four methods. As Jewish historian Dr. Barry D. Walfish notes, "Rather than being a methodology, *pardes* is a convenient way of describing the four approaches that medieval exegetes took in commenting on a biblical book."[3]

We approach all great literature, and all the more so the Bible— fountain and source of subsequent great literature—for its story line *and* as an opportunity to deepen our spiritual connections to ourselves, to each other, to the world, and to the Divine. This cascade of insight flows when we refuse to adhere to a single stream of interpretation and remain willing to shuttle along multiple paths, engaging heart, mind, and soul in the process. The approaches of PARDES create that possibility for purified emotion, clarified thought, and enlightened spirit. Each approach highlights one particular way of explicating the biblical tale.

### PESHAT

**P**    Physical, "simple." This level clarifies and explains salient historical, literary, and linguistic building blocks found in a literal reading of the Scripture. Whatever other, more multivalent approaches a person also uses, *peshat* remains crucial, as the Talmud reminds us: "No passage loses its *peshat*" (Shabbat 63a; Yevamot 24a).

## REMEZ

R  Intellectual, "hint." This level of reading focuses on allegorical, philosophical interpretations. It uncovers implied meanings hidden under the surface, broader principles derived from the concrete passages, and makes visible the implied concepts in the text and in our reading. *Remez* involves cross-references to other texts.

## DERASH

D  Emotional, "search." This level of reading delves into homiletic, ethical, religious, legal interpretations and is rooted in Rabbinic creative, associative ways of reading and intuiting the text. This layer presents the discursive, analytical, and performative faces of religion, law, and morality.

## SOD

S  Spiritual, "hidden." This level of reading involves mystical, symbolic, anagogic interpretations. Here we can peer at the theosophical, contemplative, symbolic layer of meaning. We can also bring those subversive, hidden meanings buried deep in the text and in our consciousness to the surface.

By allowing each approach to retain its own focus and integrity, we enable ourselves to grow in diverse ways without forcing ourselves to follow coercive social norms or artificially conform to others' views.

These four approaches are not competing, mutually exclusive meanings. Instead, Jewish teaching affirms that the underlying unity of God's word is mediated through the layered garments of Torah, and that "God speaks, and one hears in accordance with one's life task and spiritual level or need."[4] These complementary meanings remain open, expansive, interactive, and supple. We—the readers—make them visible by our interpretive energy, creativity, and vision, and they are offered here to help us recover the hidden treasures of Isaac's sacrifice and Abraham's test.

Following the translation and commentary, the book offers con-templative responses to life's tests, refracted through the characters, plotlines, and images in this one biblical tale. Each explores more fully a distinct challenge or implication encountered by Abraham, Isaac, Sarah, or God. Some of these responses look past this particular story to the contextual background deepening our encounters with God, Torah, life, children, and suffering—all key grounds of the trial of Abraham and the binding of Isaac, and life's tests for ourselves.

# PART ONE

# Exploring the Depths

Translation and Commentary of Genesis 22

What follows is my translation of Genesis 22, the biblical story of the trial of Abraham and the binding of Isaac, with a multilayered commentary.

To prepare for engagement, you might consider first reading the story itself a few times without looking at the commentaries, allowing the unmediated words of the Bible to directly enter your heart, your soul, and your mind. After you feel at home in the biblical tale, then you are in a position to open a dialogue with the information and varied perspectives found in the commentaries.

Each of us will choose our own path through the maze of different voices that follow, and each path is welcome. Some will want to track a particular strand of commentary all the way through; others may choose to read all the possible commentaries to a particular verse before moving on to the next one. Some may want to read all the way to the end without break; others may prefer to pause frequently to contemplate a verse before reading further.

I invite you to pick up a pen and add your own commentary in the margins, as you join your distinct voice to the conversations through the millennia swirling around this gripping tale.

I invite you to find yourself, to see yourself, to place yourself in its telling and retelling.

# Translation

1 It was after these things, God tested Abraham. He said to him, "Abraham," and he said, "Here I am." 2 He said, "Please take your son, your favored, whom you love, Isaac, and go to the land of Moriah, and offer him there as an offering on one of the mountains that I will tell you." 3 Abraham rose early in the morning, and he saddled his donkey and took two youths with him and Isaac, his son. He split the wood of his offering, and he arose and he went to the place of which God had told him. 4 On the third day Abraham lifted his eyes and saw the place from afar. 5 Abraham said to the youths, "Remain here with the donkey. I and the lad will go there; and we will worship, and we will return to you." 6 Abraham took the wood of the offering and placed it on Isaac, his son. And he took in his hand the flame and the knife; and the two walked together. 7 Isaac said to Abraham, his father, saying, "My father!" And he said, "Here I am, my son." And he said, "Here is the flame and the wood; but where is the sheep for the burnt offering?" 8 Abraham said, "God will see to the sheep for the offering, my son." And the two walked together. 9 They arrived at the place of which God had told him, and Abraham built there the altar; he arranged the wood; bound Isaac, his son; placed him on the altar, above the wood. 10 Abraham extended his hand and took the knife to slaughter his son. 11 An angel of

the Lord called to him from the heavens and said, "Abraham! Abraham!" He said, "Here I am." 12 He said, "Do not send your hand against the lad, and do nothing to him. For now I know that you fear God, and have not withheld your son, your favored, from Me." 13 Abraham lifted his eyes and saw, and, behold! Another ram was caught in a bush by his horns. Abraham went and took the ram and offered it as an offering in place of his son. 14 Abraham called the name of the place "the Lord sees," as they say today, "On the mount of the Lord is vision." 15 The angel of the Lord called to Abraham a second time from the heavens. 16 He said, "By Myself I swear, proclaims the Lord: Because you have done this thing and not withheld your son, your favored, 17 I will surely bless and multiply your seed as the stars of the heavens and the sand that is by the lips of the sea; and your seed shall seize the gates of their enemies. 18 All the peoples of the earth shall bless themselves by your seed, because you heeded My voice." 19 Abraham returned to his youths, and they arose and went together to Be'er-Sheba; and Abraham remained at Be'er-Sheba.

# Commentary

## VERSE 1

It was after these things, God tested Abraham. He said to him, "Abraham," and he said, "Here I am."

### It was after these things

**P** Some time after the expulsion of Ishmael, which happened when Isaac was three years old.

**R** There are always hidden roots—precedents that shape our present, events and people long past, our memories of whom constrain our present and our future. Often we don't even recall the events, can't even name the people. "These things" unnamed and often unlabeled become the filters through which we see each other and our possibilities.

**D** Some say the phrase *these things* refers to the Accuser (*ha-Satan*) baiting God by saying that Abraham had lots of meals for guests but never offered any sacrifice to God. God retorts that Abraham wouldn't even hesitate to sacrifice Isaac. Others trace it to sibling rivalry between Ishmael and Isaac. Ishmael boasted that he was more pious and brave than Isaac because Ishmael was willing to be circumcised as an adult. Isaac insisted that he would sacrifice his whole body if asked! Yet a third source understands *these things* to refer to Abraham's treaty with Avimelekh. His reliance on intrigue and military power belied

---

P  *Peshat—literal*          R  *Remez—allegorical*

a lack of faith that called for a public reaffirmation. Our deepest tests emerge in the expression of our strongest commitments, our most embedded jealousies, or our attempts to flee from freedom and our highest values.

## God

P The Hebrew name *Elohim* identifies God in the bulk of this story (with the exception of 11–15) as the biblical source E, one of the ancient sources from which the current text of the Bible was compiled.

R Our relationship to the cosmos, to life itself, shuttles between a sense of strict consequences (justice) and emotional connection (love). The Midrash labels those two modes using two of God's names: *Elohim* signifies God in the mode of justice, and the Tetragrammaton (Y-H-V-H) signifies God in the mode of love. Here, God's justice calls Abraham to the test. Through his response (and then through God's response to that response), we will see God's love, Y-H-V-H, emerge.

S Existence and life do not answer to our moral or rational sense. Instead, we find ourselves responding to a cosmos that is indifferent, sovereign, and powerful. This awesome majesty is known in biblical language as *Elohim,* the aspect of God so transcendent that it is beyond relationship, beyond moral category, above judgment. There are many religious and spiritual authorities who pander to their followers' fear and ego by presenting God merely as a cosmic big buddy, forgiving their own foibles while condemning those of everyone else. Integrating the incompatible aspects of transcendent and immanent, unfathomable and intimate, undomesticated and accountable is at the heart of a mature and honest spiritual life.

D *Derash*—homiletic      S *Sod*—mystical

## God tested Abraham

**P**  The narrator conveys this information to the reader without letting Abraham or Isaac know that this is merely a test. We enter the story assured that Isaac will be safe. Our attention thus moves from Isaac and his well-being to Abraham and his fidelity.

**R**  Reality often confronts us with what we perceive to be tests—challenges or burdens that we neither choose nor deserve. What remains open to us is the choice of how we will respond. How we handle life's tests remains ours to decide.

Is it possible that God doesn't know how Abraham will respond to the test? Could the outcome be in question? Spiritual responsibility is grounded in radical freedom: humans are free agents capable of distinguishing good from evil, right from wrong, and are free to make a choice between them. In that sense, then, only Abraham can determine what his response will be, and even God can't know that response in advance. Or, alternatively, the test is to show the world that it is possible to sacrifice one's all for an ideal; it is possible for human beings to put everything on the line for what they believe. Abraham's test was to show this possibility so that others would learn from it and emulate it. It is, after all, a story in the world's best-selling book! Through that telling, we are all witnesses, as it were, to Abraham's trial and Isaac's binding.

**D**  Pirkei Avot tells us that God tested Abraham ten times, but this test—the last of the ten—is the only one explicitly labeled as a test. Life's tests—the opportunities to show ourselves capable of rising to the highest standards—often come unannounced and unlabeled. Recognizing that a challenge or a tragedy is also an opportunity for community, faith, or personal growth is itself the first step in passing the test.

**S**  The Hebrew word for test, *nes*, can also mean "banner" or something elevated high above. In that sense, this is not a test (as in

---

**P**  *Peshat—literal*    **R**  *Remez—allegorical*

a trial) but an opportunity for Abraham to elevate himself to a higher spiritual level. Often, life's tribulations are precisely the arenas in which spiritual growth can occur and are often the very occasions when that spiritual greatness, now actualized, becomes a source of public inspiration and resolve.

## "Abraham"

P   God calls Abraham's name only once, whereas elsewhere in this story the name is proclaimed twice—by the angel—as an expression of intimacy and of haste.

D   Perhaps the reason God only calls out "Abraham" once is to avoid throwing him into a panic. By allowing him to remain calm, God gives Abraham the emotional space to make a free and deliberate decision.

## "Here I am"

P   These are Abraham's only words to God throughout this entire story, indicating his attention and readiness.

D   When we become aware of the Ultimate, all we can respond with is the totality of our presence, our attention, and our willingness to be in that presence. Abraham offers only that, because there is nothing else to offer.

*Hineni* (Here I am) is also an expression of humility.

---

D   *Derash—homiletic*     S   *Sod—mystical*

## VERSE 2

He said, "Please take your son, your favored, whom you love, Isaac, and go to the land of Moriah, and offer him there as an offering on one of the mountains that I will tell you."

### "Please take your son"

P   *Na* (please) is an untranslatable Hebrew word that transforms a command into a polite question, like "if you please" in English. With the addition of the adverb *na*, the harsh imperative becomes a request, highlighting Abraham's liberty to accept or refuse the test.

D   So it is with power. Even when framed as a request, there is only one correct answer. Perhaps, though, we are meant to learn a lesson from the opposite perspective—that the measure of real authority is the graciousness with which those less powerful are treated.

### "your favored"

P   In other translations, this is rendered as "your only one," but Genesis has already told us that Abraham has another son, Ishmael. The Hebrew *yachid* signifies specialness, favor, heightening the enormity of what Abraham is asked to give up. Does this term also signify the one selected to inherit the covenant?

On the other hand, according to the *peshat* of the narrative, Abraham had previously banished Hagar and Ishmael, so Isaac is—both legally and in relationship—his only remaining son.

D   *Favored* and *loved* are listed separately. The one favored with visible signs of preference—status, grades, trophies, income, and fame—may not be the one most deserving of love or the one who feels sufficiently loved. Isaac is both the heir of the covenant and also the most beloved child.

---

P   *Peshat—literal*       R   *Remez—allegorical*

## "whom you love"

P The whirlpool of words swirls ever tighter around the very son Abraham most adores and would be least willing to surrender. This is the Bible's first use of the verb *to love*, strikingly invoked in reference to the parent-child bond.

## "Isaac"

P Finally the son's identity is specified by name! There is no more room for evasion. In Hebrew, Isaac's name, paradoxically, means "He shall laugh."

S Perverse, indeed, that the one called "Laughter" is shocked into terrified silence in this most trying of ordeals.

## "go to the land"

P This echoes the command by which God instructed Abraham to leave his father's home and travel toward Israel. This is another journey undertaken without knowing the precise outcome.

D His two most important trips: the first, terminating the heritage of his parents' pagan culture and influence, and the second, terminating his destiny through his son. Go, *lekh lekha*, is an assertion of our existential aloneness. We enter the world alone, and we leave it alone.

## "Moriah"

P Never mentioned again in the Bible, this place name could mean "to see," or it could mean "to fear," or, perhaps, "to teach." It is possible that all three meanings are intended simultaneously. *Moriah* refers to an ancient and well-known site of worship. Abraham knows where it is, tells the lads that he is going to "*the* place" to worship, and builds "*the* altar" there, as though it is a well-known altar.

---

D *Derash—homiletic*    S *Sod—mystical*

## "offer him there as an offering"

P   God's words are ambiguous. The Hebrew literally means "lift up," as in "lift him onto the altar." Abraham hears the command as a command to sacrifice his son. Technically, all God has demanded is that Abraham place Isaac on the altar.

## "I will tell you"

P   As with Creation, God's primary mode of intervention is the spoken word.

## VERSE 3

Abraham rose early in the morning, and he saddled his donkey and took two youths with him and Isaac, his son. He split the wood of his offering, and he arose and he went to the place of which God had told him.

### Abraham rose early in the morning

P  Abraham has no verbal response to God's command. In silence, he awakens with alacrity, and in silence he goes about preparing for and beginning the journey. His early rising echoes his similar obedience when commanded to expel Hagar and Ishmael (Genesis 21:14).

D  According to Midrash, Abraham spent much of the evening persuading his wife, Sarah, to consent to his journey with Isaac. He told her that he was taking Isaac to an academy to learn Torah on a higher level, and she gave her permission for that purpose. He rose early in the morning so she wouldn't have an opportunity to change her mind.

Abraham's early rising is a sign of his eagerness to obey the command. He literally rises to his duty as he knows it.

S  Anytime we see our ethical obligations or our emotional possibilities and we make them our priority, we rise—spiritually, ethically, or emotionally. Each time we recognize our duty and evade it or make excuses for postponing it, we diminish ourselves.

### he saddled his donkey

P  He does this himself, as he does the other menial chores for the journey, to accentuate his obedience to the divine command.

D  Love shatters rules, the Talmud notes (Sanhedrin 105b). Normally, a great man doesn't saddle pack animals himself; he lets

---

D  *Derash—homiletic*      S  *Sod—mystical*

his servants do that work. But so great is Abraham's love (for Isaac? for God?) that he takes on the task eagerly and willingly. Don't we also, when motivated by love, gladly perform acts of service we might otherwise delegate to others?

## took two youths with him

P Their role is to assist along the way. The Hebrew for *youth*, *na'ar*, need not mean someone chronologically young, but can refer to someone who renders service, an attendant.

## and Isaac, his son

P Again, the name Isaac comes toward the end of the sentence to heighten the drama and focus our attention on Isaac's sacrifice.

D Perhaps Isaac is postponed to the very last to help us feel Abraham's hesitation and ambivalence in having to bring his son for this purpose.

## He split the wood of his offering

P Omitting no detail, Abraham is prepared to fulfill God's will.

S The verb for *splitting the wood* is the same verb used for God splitting the sea when Abraham's descendants leave Egypt to find freedom. The two acts are connected on a spiritual level: Abraham attends to the details of implementing God's will, and God attends to the details of Abraham's descendants.

## he arose and he went

R Accomplishing something great requires great strength. Abraham does not hesitate or quiver in weakness. He rises up to accomplish what he has resolved to do. Excessive self-doubt can undermine even the most worthy undertaking.

---

P *Peshat*—literal   R *Remez*—allegorical

## VERSE 4

On the third day Abraham lifted his eyes and saw the place from afar.

### On the third day

**P** The days separating the initial command and the subsequent arrival at Moriah emphasize Abraham's steely determination to obey. His response is no fleeting impulse.

**S** The third day is also the day that revelation took place at Mount Sinai (Exodus 19:11), another fateful mountain in the spiritual consciousness of humanity. This, too, is an opportunity to encounter God at a deeper, more primal level than is normally accessible. The third day is also the limit to how long a sacrifice may remain uneaten (Leviticus 7:17). Perhaps we learn here that the real sacrifice began when Abraham was called to offer Isaac and ended three days later at Mount Moriah when God substituted the ram for the boy.

### Abraham lifted his eyes and saw

**P** The next time Abraham lifts his eyes and sees (verse 13), the trial will be over.

**D** Our vision is often constrained by our expectations or our fears. Abraham dreads seeing the place where this trial must occur, yet, looking up, that is precisely what he sees.

### the place

**P** The Land of Moriah, or the place of sacrifice on Mount Moriah.

**S** The Hebrew, *Ha-Makom,* is a euphemism for God, who is "the place of the world, even though the world is not God's place" (*Bereshit Rabbah* 8:10). God is the ground of all being. Abraham

---

**D** *Derash—homiletic*      **S** *Sod—mystical*

looks up and recognizes this moment and this occasion as an encounter with the Divine. But whereas sacrifice is a time to draw near (the literal meaning of *korban*, sacrifice, is "to draw near"), this one is still from afar.

## from afar

P Seeing his destination must have heightened Abraham's horror, intensifying an already excruciating trial.

## VERSE 5

> Abraham said to the youths, "Remain here with the donkey. I and the lad will go there; and we will worship, and we will return to you."

### Remain here

P  The sacrifice is to be private, linking father and son.

D  Each of us is the star in our own drama, the central figure in the stories of those closest to us, and a mere extra and backdrop to the vast majority of those whose paths we cross. These two nameless boys are marginal, so much so that they cannot move ahead. They remain stuck where they are, even though this extraordinary event is about to take place. They do not witness it.

### with the donkey

S  How easy it is to sleepwalk through life, moving from chore to chore, attending only to our wants and desires, like a human caricature of a beast of burden. We all have the propensity to give in to the reflexive nature of habit, fear, and want, rather than to muster the vision and consciousness to savor the days and to live in the moment. Abraham's servants, even though accompanying the two patriarchs, miss the sacred moment through inattention. If we were there, would we, too, remain with the donkey? Or would we lift our eyes and see *Ha-Makom*?

### we will return to you

P  Abraham's remark to the servant boys conceals the impending sacrifice from Isaac, while reminding us that the outcome is different from what Abraham anticipates.

---

D  *Derash—homiletic*          S  *Sod—mystical*

S   There is a power in our words, often beyond our conscious awareness. Hence, many of the world's spiritual traditions encourage
practitioners to refrain from making negative comments and
instead train themselves to issue gratuitous blessings. In Hebrew,
the word for *word* is *davar*, which also means "thing." Words are
things that enter the world through our mouths—and they have
a surprising ability to create their own reality, even when it's
unanticipated.

## VERSE 6

Abraham took the wood of the offering and placed it on Isaac, his son. And he took in his hand the flame and the knife; and the two walked together.

### took the wood ... and placed it on Isaac, his son

P Isaac replaces the donkey as beast of burden. Incidentally, while the text does not specify Isaac's age at the time of the sacrifice, he had to be old enough to bear the weight of the wood.

D Some say Isaac was a strapping thirty-seven years old at the time. Others say that he was twenty-six. None of the classical sources see him as a young boy.

How often do we carry our own emotional baggage with us into new situations where it need not intrude? How often do we bring with us the seeds of our own undoing?

Is Abraham imposing this unusual practice on his son in order to provoke him to ask about the sacrifice?

### he took in his hand

P Abraham carries the dangerous implements himself, minimizing the possibility of Isaac becoming blemished prior to the sacrifice.

D A remarkable father even now, Abraham insists on caring for his son's well-being within the context of the trial. He may have to sacrifice his son, but no other harm will come to his boy. This loving gesture—foolish in the eyes of strict rationality—reflects the complex, maddening care that parents often bestow on their children.

---

D *Derash—homiletic*     S *Sod—mystical*

### the flame

P   The *flame* could mean equipment for producing fire, such as a firestone or brazier.

### the knife

P   No ordinary knife, this rare term, *ma'akhelet*, signifies a large butcher knife.

### the two walked together

P   In silent solidarity.

## VERSE 7

> Isaac said to Abraham, his father, saying, "My father!"
> And he said, "Here I am, my son." And he said, "Here is
> the flame and the wood; but where is the sheep for the
> burnt offering?"

### Isaac said to Abraham

P Isaac breaks the silence with the only recorded conversation between him and his father.

### father ... "father"

P The repetition of this word heightens the sense of Abraham's agony, Isaac's trust, and the unbroken harmony between the two of them.

D Is Isaac calling for his father to arouse his compassion? To assure himself that he retains his father's love?

### "Here I am, my son"

P Abraham's response to Isaac is the same response he offers God, with the added endearment to comfort the boy.

D The doubt that Isaac hints to Abraham through the phrase *my father* elicits a loving answer: "my son." I still feel toward you as a father toward a son—that has not changed, nor will it.

### "where is the sheep for the burnt offering?"

P Isaac's question, presumably asked without awareness, pierces to the core of this story's extraordinary tension.

---

D *Derash*—homiletic    S *Sod*—mystical

## VERSE 8

Abraham said, "God will see to the sheep for the offering, my son." And the two walked together.

### "God will see"

**P** This response anticipates the name of the site revealed in verse 14 and plays on the pun of *yireh* as both "vision" and "fear." Its ambivalence also deflects Isaac's question.

**S** God will see, not Abraham. It is not Abraham who has determined Isaac's role, but God who has assigned both Abraham and Isaac's role in this cosmic drama. Instead of asking ourselves what we demand out of life's situations, can we shift our attention to ask what it is that God wants of us? Can we retrain our hearts to view each person before us as a messenger bearing a message intended uniquely for us, to approach each challenge as a lesson designed to teach us precisely the lesson we next need to learn?

### "my son"

**P** Frequently repeated throughout as a sign of tenderness and affection.

### the two walked together

**P** Repeated for the second time (see verse 6). The solidarity between Abraham and Isaac remains strong.

**R** It is easy to have a sense of solidarity when you're ignorant of impending reality. Yet this questioning and responding indicate that Abraham was able to allude to the unparalleled sacrifice ahead, and Isaac gets it. Now their "walking together" is that much more significant. Knowing what life will bring, they still remain united in purpose.

---

**P** *Peshat—literal*          **R** *Remez—allegorical*

## VERSE 9

They arrived at the place of which God had told him, and Abraham built there the altar; he arranged the wood; bound Isaac, his son; placed him on the altar, above the wood.

### the place ... the altar

P The definite article (*the*) indicates that this is a well-known place and that Abraham is using a well-established altar.

### bound

P The Hebrew *akkad* is used here, which in the Talmud is a technical term for binding the front and hind legs of an animal.

S Could Abraham possibly have bound his adult son, Isaac, without his consent? How often in our own lives do we cede our freedom to others because we attribute to them authority, influence, or an understanding beyond our own? In fact, we usually don't have to abandon our own inner sense of integrity, style, or priority. Isaac allows himself to be bound, faithful to his own path. Can we hold onto our own inner light despite the many social pressures seeking to snuff it out?

### built ... arranged ... bound ... placed ... extended ... took

P This staccato series of verbs that stretches throughout verses 9 and 10 advances the action with a jarring and relentless pace. There is no hesitation, just as there are no words.

D Before, the two had walked together. Now Abraham acts alone. There are moments in life when we must take full responsibility and simply act—in advance of consensus—with or without the support or understanding of those around us.

---

D *Derash*—homiletic          S *Sod*—mystical

## VERSE 10

Abraham extended his hand and took the knife to slaughter his son.

### to slaughter

R   We already know that his intention is to slaughter Isaac, so why tell us the obvious? To underscore the principle that acts of sacrifice require intention. Whereas some acts are valid whether or not they are deliberate, acts of spiritual devotion (or emotional devotion, for that matter) require conscious intention.

### his son

P   Once again, the sentence ends with the relationship, heightening our anticipation and emphasizing the strength of Abraham's feelings for Isaac.

D   Even at this moment of most intense drama, Isaac's concern extends toward his aged father. He worries how his father will be able to tell his mother the grim news of his death and what will become of both of them in their old age without their son to care for them.

S   Abraham looks down and sees his son, but Isaac looks up, toward the heavens. Isaac sees the angels, weeping at his father's act of faith and his act of selfless sacrifice and devotion. The tears of the weeping angels drip into Isaac's eyes, forever changing his vision. To see the heavens weep at one's misfortune and one's sacrifice is a level of cosmic solidarity that transcends all human bonds. It is to be at one with all creation, without requiring a false assurance that all will be well in the end.

---

P   *Peshat—literal*          R   *Remez—allegorical*

## VERSE 11

An angel of the LORD called to him from the heavens and said, "Abraham! Abraham!" He said, "Here I am."

### An angel of the LORD called to him

**P** Generally nameless, angels in the Bible are embodiments of a divine message (the Hebrew, *malakh*, comes from the verb "to send"). They fulfill the mandate and have no other identity or existence. One might, perhaps, translate *angel* as "messenger," or even "message," in this case, from God.

**S** The angel proclaims, but it is quickly apparent that it is God who is speaking. As the ancient Midrash (*Va-Yikra Rabbah* 1:9) declares, "The angel calls, but it is the Divine Word that speaks." God's message is clothed in many different garments.

### the LORD

**P** After the trial is over, God is no longer *Elohim* in the story, but appears using God's four-letter name—the Tetragrammaton, Y-H-V-H. The sudden shift of God's name and other linguistic-literary features leads many contemporary scholars to identify verses 11–14 as from another source, RJE (Redactor of J and E).

**S** Y-H-V-H is the name associated with God's mercy. No longer focused on strict justice, God's mercy breaks through to bring Isaac off the altar and to permit Abraham to lower his arm.

### called to him from the heavens

**P** Angels generally shuttle back and forth between the heavens and earth (as with Jacob's ladder, Genesis 28:12), but the pressing need for immediate intervention precludes that travel, so the angel has to call out from the heavens rather than make a personal appearance.

---

**D** *Derash—homiletic*          **S** *Sod—mystical*

## "Abraham! Abraham!"

P  The repetition of Abraham's name is both a sign of intimacy with God and a sign of urgency.

R  Four biblical leaders had the honor of being called twice: Abraham, Jacob (Genesis 46:2), Moses (Exodus 3:4), and Samuel (1 Samuel 3:10). Lest we despair that such greatness only existed in the ancient past, the Midrash assures us that every generation contains such spiritual giants. These four men exemplify virtues: generosity, service, learning, and justice. Humanity is built on such a fourfold base.

D  When commanded to sacrifice Isaac, calling Abraham's name once sufficed. But now that he is fixated on fulfilling that commandment, it requires repeating his name twice to get him to stop. We often get so accustomed to how we've always acted, to the way we're supposed to behave, that it takes something drastic to create the possibility of fresh thinking or a new approach, even though it is clearly called for once we've broken with the constraints of habit or previous expectation.

   According to mystical thought, the angel calls Abraham's name twice to create his soul anew—now inspired with a new heart and new courage.

## "Here I am"

P  For the third time, Abraham's response indicates complete attentiveness and willingness to respond.

D  One ancient source understands this third *Hineni* as the moment that Abraham refuses to descend from the altar unless God promises to reciprocate Abraham's faithful loyalty by promising to absolve the people of Israel, should they sin in the future. Indeed, God promises to think of the altar as though Isaac's ashes were still strewn on the altar and to forgive the people of Israel when they repent.

P  *Peshat—literal*    R  *Remez—allegorical*

## VERSE 12

> He said, "Do not send your hand against the lad, and do nothing to him. For now I know that you fear God, and have not withheld your son, your favored, from Me."

### He

P   God? The angel?

### "Do not send your hand … and do nothing to him"

P   First expressed as a prohibition (negative), then as an imperative (positive); it is not uncommon for biblical commandments to be presented twice, as both prohibition and imperative.

R   As is often true in life, the meaning of an action does not simply lie in the action itself, but also in the intention that motivates the behavior. Smiling can reflect affection or betrayal; killing can be a matter of murder or self-defense. Meaning is found in the context and intentions underlying the action. In Abraham's case, *mitzvah* (commandment, connection, good deed) is not at the level of behavior, but in responding to and implementing God's will. At one point, putting Isaac on the altar is a *mitzvah*, and refusing would be both rupture and rebellion. Now, taking him off the altar is a *mitzvah*, and keeping him there would constitute rebellion.

### "now I know"

P   This is not an issue of divine knowledge, but a recognition that what was merely potential must become actual. Abraham has now earned the label "God fearer" through his determination to walk the walk.

D   Or, "now it is known." Your willingness to bind and sacrifice Isaac will become one of the world's foundational stories, inspiring countless generations to a willingness to sacrifice for their highest ideals.

D   *Derash—homiletic*          S   *Sod—mystical*

## "fear God"

P    *Yirei Elohim.* The Hebrew continues the ambiguous wordplay around fear and seeing (since *yirah* can be read as "fear" or as "seeing"). Here, fear is not simply an emotion, but an attitude that is demonstrated through action.

R    *Fear* here cannot mean fear of consequences, which is a lower fear. What possible consequences could have been more stark than the sacrifice of his son, the obliteration of all Abraham had worked for his entire life, the end of the covenant, and people accusing him of hypocrisy and murder? Fear of consequences is held to be unworthy of a spiritually striving soul. Instead, the higher fear is a reverence inspired by God's radical greatness, by the marvel of life itself, by the sheer wonder of being. Abraham manifests that higher fear, and that makes him a worthy model for us all.

S    *Fear* as reverence is not the opposite of love, it is an outgrowth of love. Just as we marvel at the starry skies or beam at a loved one who accomplishes a goal, so Abraham's character is one of love for God and love for God's children. Reverence and love interact dynamically to keep each other dynamic and transformative.

## "your son, your favored"

P    Here, God repeats the description of Isaac from the story's beginning. Abraham got it right: Isaac was, indeed, the son God wanted to be elevated and brought close.

## "from Me"

P    Because angels are merely messengers of God, personifications of God's will, they often transform into God midway through a conversation (with Hagar [Genesis 21:19], prior to Sodom's destruction [Genesis 18:33], at the burning bush [Exodus 3:4], and here). Abraham now finds himself listening directly to God.

---

P   *Peshat—literal*      R   *Remez—allegorical*

## VERSE 13

Abraham lifted his eyes and saw, and, behold! Another ram was caught in a bush by his horns. Abraham went and took the ram and offered it as an offering in place of his son.

### Abraham lifted his eyes and saw

P The last time Abraham "lifted his eyes and saw" was prior to this terrible trial (verse 4). It is now safely over, and he can again lift his eyes, this time to a vision of salvation and triumph rather than agony and challenge.

R Perhaps the ram was there all along, but Abraham never lifted his eyes because he was trapped by his course of action or because he had abandoned hope of any alternative. Once he could not simply follow through on his sacrificial mission, he had to find an alternative, and no sooner was he looking for an alternative then there it was!

### Another ram

P Earlier manuscripts read "one [echad] ram," rather than "another [achar] ram," because of confusion between two similar Hebrew letters, resh (ר) and dalet (ד).

D It is to remember (and commemorate) the binding of Isaac and Abraham's trial that Jews blow a shofar (a ram's horn) on Rosh Ha-Shanah, the New Year festival, to crown God as sovereign.

### Abraham went and took the ram

P Abraham assumes that God sent the ram as a substitute sacrifice for his son, even though God never says that.

---

D Derash—homiletic    S Sod—mystical

## in place of his son

S    The phrase indicates that, in some important way, the rituals of sacrifice are substitutionary, that the animal serves in our stead: its life for our life, its terror marking our terror, its flesh and blood reality reminding us of our own embodiedness. Today, reading about the ancient sacrifices serves a similar purpose for Jews and Muslims (who read of the sacrifice of Ishmael instead of Isaac), and the vicarious sacrifice of Jesus is understood to function in a similar way for Christians.

## VERSE 14

Abraham called the name of the place "the LORD sees,"
as they say today, "On the mount of the LORD is vision."

### the LORD sees

P Abraham names the site after his earlier response to Isaac, which turns out to be prophetic in ways he hadn't known at the time. In verse 8 he said, *Elohim yireh* (God sees). Now he names the place *Y-H-V-H Yireh* (the LORD sees).

S Or, more literally, "God will see," meaning God will seek a place for those among us whom seek out the Divine. That place, from the *Akedah* to the present, is the Mount of Vision, Mount Zion in Jerusalem.

### as they say today

P A saying popular at the time the story was put in writing, based on this story.

### On the mount of the LORD ... vision

P A reference to Mount Zion, the Temple Mount in Jerusalem. The Septuagint translates this verse as "On the mount the LORD appears."

S Or, perhaps, on the mount of the LORD, we appear. Our presence, our willingness to stand up and be counted among the forces for righteousness, justice, compassion, and inclusion signifies that we have internalized the values of Abraham's love and Isaac's willingness to serve. Living such a life is the sure sign of being among the children of Abraham.

---

 D  *Derash—homiletic*    S  *Sod—mystical*

## VERSE 15

The angel of the LORD called to Abraham a second time from the heavens.

### The angel of the LORD

P Back to an angel, as there is another message on the way.

### a second time from the heavens

P This time the message is a reward for Abraham's passing the test.

## VERSE 16

He said, "By Myself I swear, proclaims the LORD: Because you have done this thing and not withheld your son, your favored,

### He said

P  The messenger's voice, not just the content of the message, is God's.

### "By Myself I swear"

P  To underscore the significance of these (now earned) blessings, God invokes an oath, swearing on God's own being. This oath is irrevocable.

### "proclaims the LORD"

P  A prophetic formula again underscoring the binding significance of the promise.

### "Because you have done this thing"

P  Previously, God's promises to Abraham were acts of unmerited grace. Now, after the trial/sacrifice, Abraham is rewarded for his fidelity and obedience.

---

D  *Derash*—homiletic          S  *Sod*—mystical

## VERSE 17

I will surely bless and multiply your seed as the stars of
the heavens and the sand that is by the lips of the sea;
and your seed shall seize the gates of their enemies.

### "I will surely bless"

P    This is a reiteration of previous blessings, with two new twists:
the imagery of sand and of taking our enemies' gates.

R    The Hebrew indicates emphasis by doubling the Hebrew verb,
*barekh avarekhekha*. The mystics read the two verbs to indicate
present and future: I will bless you in the present, and I shall
bless your progeny in the future.

### "sand that is by the lips of the sea"

P    A new metaphor for the multitudes that will descend from
Abraham.

### "seize the gates of their enemies"

P    Abraham's descendants are promised military triumph over
their foes.

---

P  *Peshat*—literal      R  *Remez*—allegorical

## VERSE 18

All the peoples of the earth shall bless themselves by your seed, because you heeded My voice."

### "All the peoples … shall bless themselves by your seed"

P    An allusion to Genesis 12:3 ("I will bless those who bless you / And curse him that curses you") and 18:18 ("All the nations of the earth are to bless themselves through him"), now expressed as prophecy—not only will blessing themselves by Abraham's descendants be efficacious, but people will actually do it!

### "because you heeded My voice"

P    Being the source of blessing to humanity is a consequence of obedience to God's command.

S    Abraham heeded God's voice so thoroughly that no further spiritual-ethical elevation was possible. Consequently, no conversation between God and Abraham is ever recorded again. God's voice is always an opportunity for growth, often in the guise of a trial or challenge.

D    *Derash*—homiletic          S    *Sod*—mystical

## VERSE 19

Abraham returned to his youths, and they arose and
went together to Be'er–Sheba; and Abraham remained
at Be'er-Sheba.

## Abraham returned to his youths

P Does this include Isaac or not? The text is ambiguous, since both
Isaac and the two servant boys have been referred to by this same
term previously.

D Apparently, Abraham returns without Isaac. Some scholars understand that Isaac really was sacrificed in the original telling of the
story (E); hence Abraham has to return alone. In the present telling, of course, Isaac is still alive, so their separation is even more
poignant. They never converse or see each other in this life again.

## arose and went together

P This time it is not father and son who proceed together, but
patriarch and servants.

D Despite the remarkable encounter with the Divine, Abraham
holds himself to be no better than the two youths. In spirit, he
walks together with them, and with all humanity.

S Despite the traumatic near-sacrifice of his son, Abraham is still
able to return to life. The miracle in our own time—of Holocaust survivors (and other survivors of tragedy and trauma) who
go on to create new families, raise children, pursue productive
lives—is the resurgent tenacity of the human soul. Such staunch
vitality is worthy of notice—in Abraham's time and in our own.

---

# PART TWO

# Deepening Our Encounters

## Reflections on Life's Tests in Genesis 22

We have honored the integrity of the Torah's telling and gleaned what wisdom we may from approaching the story of Isaac's binding as a coherent unit. The translation of the story created a space for the flow of the plot and the spare, stark vigor of its prose. The commentary helped us attend to seams and provocations within the telling, slowing us down to truly notice, to savor, to taste, but always within the context of the story as presented by the Torah itself. As is fitting, the first engagements are on the Torah's turf—with the flow and rhythm established by the visions of the Bible's coherence and integrity.

Now that the biblical story and the fourfold commentary are under our belts, we are poised to dive more deeply. Biblical stories project the depths of our human nature in story form, displaying the challenges, struggles, and glories of humanity in intimate and unvarnished candor.

At this stage of the journey, we kick free from the structure of the narrative itself and read the story not from the outside in (with the Bible's priorities at the forefront) but from the inside out (with our own personality, issues, shortcomings, and strengths at the center). How the trial of Abraham, the binding of Isaac, looks from the inside, when we wrap it around our own existential concerns like a warm blanket, when we gaze at our own life struggles through the lenses of this ancient, stunning tale—this is the next step in our pilgrimage.

This time around, the agenda is our own. The tool for illuminating our path is the Torah. Let us walk together.

# Mortality

## What You Learn When You're Under the Knife

All of us have, on occasion, experienced a period in which time itself stands still, when the normal pulsing heartbeat of the world seems suspended and the rhythmic breath of life is hushed. At such moments our perception of the world is jolted, and we see life in a new way, as if for the first time. These are moments that offer insight, occasions when we might develop a new profundity and a deeper wisdom if we are open to the opportunity.

The tale of the binding of Isaac presents a figure who could respond to that moment with such radical insight, a moment that forever altered his personality and his future. Traditionally, Isaac is known merely as the son of Abraham and the father of Jacob. He has few deeds to plead his cause as one of the founding ancestors of the children of Israel.

The Bible tells us little about Isaac's childhood. We know that he was the beloved progeny of his parents' old age. We know also that his father, Abraham, was the leader of a powerful clan, forever conducting diplomacy and warfare with local rulers, with the Pharaoh of Egypt, and even with God directly. We don't see Abraham as a loving husband or an involved father. Like other prominent leaders, he is preoccupied with important affairs on behalf of his group. Abraham's greatness lies in being the first patriarch and in spreading an awareness of the one Creator of the Universe.

Isaac's mother, Sarah, also appears as an extraordinary woman—running an enormous household, managing the servants, chiding her husband, and herself conducting several conversations with God. Sarah's greatness lies in her being the first matriarch.

Everything in Isaac's youth points to a future of public prominence and of communal leadership. We expect Isaac to be like his parents. Later generations of Jews, not finding evidence of public greatness, see Isaac as the least of Israel's founding ancestors, as little more than a link. In making that assessment, posterity fails to appreciate Isaac as an individual of deep insight and character. Later generations simply apply the wrong standards—external standards of prowess, wit, and oratory.

Isaac turns away from a life of public leadership because of one transforming event—because of the binding.

## Moments That Change Us Forever

God decides to test Abraham, the public leader, by ordering him to sacrifice his beloved son. Ever obedient to his God, Abraham responds immediately. With his son and two servants, Abraham gathers the necessary supplies and marches to a still-undesignated place to do God's bidding. "He bound Isaac, his son" (Genesis 22:9). Then Abraham takes up the knife to slay his son. Only at the last moment does an angel of God order Abraham to stop. A substitute for Isaac, a young ram caught in a bush, appears and is sacrificed instead.

The Torah reports the *Akedah* primarily as an event in Abraham's life. The narrator's intention is to show the important virtue of the fear of heaven and, secondarily, perhaps, to record God's disapproval of human sacrifice.

We are never told how Isaac responds. Indeed, once the ram appears in the thicket, the Torah's interest in Isaac seems to dissipate completely. Read superficially, the Torah implies that the binding did not affect Isaac at all—his life appears unchanged. We don't see Isaac again until his father has found a bride for the boy, yet another event recounted because of Abraham's involvement, rather than revealing any direct interest in Isaac himself.

What happens to Isaac during his ordeal on the altar? What does he see when he is under the knife? For a brief and agonizing moment, Isaac comes face-to-face with the reality of his own mortality, with the certain knowledge that he will someday die. Such an insight must permanently affect the perspective of any human being. It must forever change a person's priorities and conduct.

## Lessons from Life-Threatening Challenges

We see instances of deepened perception emerging from moments of crisis in ancient tales and in daily life itself. In 1987, during my final summer as a rabbinical student, I was a chaplain at Memorial Sloan-Kettering Cancer Center in Manhattan. I functioned as rabbi and counselor for cancer and AIDS patients on three floors of the hospital. My job was to walk into the rooms of people I had never previously met, introduce myself, and talk with them about their fears, their concerns, and their pain. Mostly, my job was to listen and to empathize.

Like Isaac, the people in Sloan-Kettering were, in a sense, under the knife. They, too, were experiencing their own mortality—a reality that the rest of us deny for as long as we can. Some patients, like Isaac, got a reprieve. Some were not so fortunate. How does such a brush with death change someone? Can we even speak of insights gained in such a terrible moment?

The Bible helps us to understand that we can. The portrait painted of Isaac is so distinctive, so unlike that of any other biblical leader, that we are justified in assuming that only some unique and overpowering event could have molded his character in such a special way.

## Isaac's Character

When next we see Isaac after the binding, the Torah reports, "He is walking in the fields" (Genesis 24:63). The Midrash understands that Isaac is reciting the afternoon prayers, *Minchah*, in the words of the psalmist, "communing with his heart and searching his soul" (Psalm 77:7). Walking quietly, lost in a world of thought and contemplation, is something we have not seen in a biblical figure, and not something we shall see again. Isaac has become more attuned to an inner life than was his father or his mother.

Isaac also relates to others in an unprecedented way. He marries Rebecca, and the Torah tells us "he loved her" (Genesis 24:67). In itself, Isaac's ability to love is rare. Only one other husband-and-wife couple, Jacob and Rachel, are described as loving each other in the entire Bible. For a man in antiquity to care so deeply for a woman is striking and noteworthy. In fact, Isaac loves his wife so deeply that he intervenes with God when his wife becomes barren. The Bible says, "Isaac pleaded with the LORD on behalf of his wife, because she was barren" (25:21). No other biblical figure is able to empathize to this degree. Isaac so identifies with his wife's suffering that he takes it on as his own.

His care for Rebecca is the fullest expression of mature intimacy. Isaac is singular among biblical figures in his ability to integrate his love for his wife with his sexual attraction for her. Isaac and Rebecca share a sexuality that is both loving and playful. The Bible tells us, "Isaac fondled his wife Rebecca" (Genesis 26:8).

Isaac is unique in the depth and seriousness of his relationship with Rebecca. This is no youthful passion, no lustful fling. Rebecca and Isaac share an adult love, the union of two souls who can be fully themselves in each other's presence. They share each other's sorrows and they learn to laugh with each other. Theirs is the Torah's truest romance.

But Isaac's insight extends beyond the realm of love. He is also a man of peace. Three times he digs wells of water, and three times those wells are contested by Philistine chieftains. Each time, Isaac cedes his wells rather than wage war.

Ben Zoma, an early Rabbinic figure, asks, "Who is rich? One who is happy with his portion" (Pirkei Avot 4:1). Isaac does not measure wealth by the number of wells he possesses or even how much money he stockpiles. His life, his family, and the safety of his own follow-ers are worth more than a few wells of water. Having himself been

# WIN A
# $100
## GIFT
## CERTIFICATE!

Fill in this card and
mail it to us—
or fill it in online at

**jewishlights.com/
feedback.html**

—to be eligible for a
$100 gift certificate for
Jewish Lights books.

JEWISH LIGHTS PUBLISHING
SUNSET FARM OFFICES RTE 4
PO BOX 237
WOODSTOCK VT   05091-0237

Place
Stamp
Here

Fill in this card and return it to us to be eligible for our quarterly drawing for a $100 gift certificate for Jewish Lights books.

*We hope that you will enjoy this book and find it useful in enriching your life.*

Book title: _____

Your comments: _____

How you learned of this book: _____

If purchased: Bookseller _____ City _____ State _____

Please send me a free JEWISH LIGHTS Publishing catalog. I am interested in: (check all that apply)

1. ❑ Spirituality
2. ❑ Mysticism/Kabbalah
3. ❑ Philosophy/Theology
4. ❑ History/Politics

5. ❑ Women's Interest
6. ❑ Environmental Interest
7. ❑ Healing/Recovery
8. ❑ Children's Books

9. ❑ Caregiving/Grieving
10. ❑ Ideas for Book Groups
11. ❑ Religious Education Resources
12. ❑ Interfaith Resources

Name (PRINT) _____

Street _____

City _____ State _____ Zip _____

E-MAIL (FOR SPECIAL OFFERS ONLY) _____

Please send a JEWISH LIGHTS Publishing catalog to my friend:

Name (PRINT) _____

Street _____

City _____ State _____ Zip _____

## JEWISH LIGHTS PUBLISHING

Tel: (802) 457-4000 • Fax: (802) 457-4004

**Available at better booksellers. Visit us online at www.jewishlights.com**

offered on an altar, Isaac is not going to sacrifice young lives for material wealth. Isaac is a man who knows the profound value of peace.

Isaac's commitment to peace is well rewarded. After he permits the Philistines to claim his wells for the final time, God blesses him and makes him prosper. The Philistines are taught a lesson in human kindness and priorities by Isaac's behavior. Impressed by his grandeur and magnanimity, they seek out Isaac and exchange oaths of friendship with him.

Ben Zoma has wisdom to offer here, too: "Who is mighty? One who conquers his evil impulse, as it is written, 'One who is slow to anger is better than he who conquers a city' [Proverbs 16:32]" (Pirkei Avot 4:1). *Avot de-Rabbi Natan*, a later commentary, adds that wisdom consists of transforming an enemy into a friend (38a). In converting the Philistines into allies and friends, Isaac demonstrates that special wisdom.

Isaac's steadfast faithfulness, his commitment to maintaining a relationship, extends even to the land of his birth. Alone of all the patriarchs, Isaac never leaves the Land of Israel. Even in time of famine, Isaac's attachment to the Land of Israel never wavers. He expresses his relationship to the land by never leaving it, and he cultivates that attachment by being the first patriarch to engage in agriculture. Both of those facts require a depth of commitment, patience, and a level of maturity that are rare even in our day.

Isaac possesses that solidity, fidelity, and commitment. He is a loving partner with Rebecca, a man who goes out of his way to keep peace with his neighbors, and one whose commitment to the Land of Israel and the God of Israel is total.

## Isaac's Perspective

Where does he gain that perspective?

I suggest to you that Isaac learns the importance of love, inner depth, and relationship when he is bound on the altar on Mount Moriah. Isaac looks at that glistening blade and he sees in its reflection his own eventual death. Awareness that his life would one day end changes him forever. In an instant, Isaac can see that public fame, lofty speeches, and the glitter of wealth and power are all meaningless in the face of death. The only possession of ultimate worth is the love of other people, a sense of connectedness with a community and with God, and having lived life with meaning, sensitivity, and love.

Isaac sees, in that instant, that it is possible to go through a lengthy life without ever truly living, that one can forever pursue pomp and acclaim and be, in reality, alone and poor. But a person who knows love, who deepens his or her own insight and sensitivity and character, possesses a richness beyond compare.

Isaac learns that lesson, and the Bible recounts it for our benefit in its own unique way. But Isaac is not alone in confronting his own death. Each week, countless people face the same glimpse of their own mortality and struggle to learn the same lessons about life. That summer in New York City, I watched numerous people wrestle with their cancer, and I saw them develop a new insight about how they would live differently in whatever time was left to them. Over and over, people in the hospital told me that they had indeed learned from their cancer.

The story of Isaac's binding presents an opportunity for us to grow in perspective without ourselves lying under the knife. By insisting on accepting our mortality and living a meaningful life, Isaac makes it possible for each of us to do the same.

# Paradox

## The Enduring Covenant

Ll of us live with unresolved polarities. Opposite perceptions of the world, each appropriate to a specific situation, jostle our sense of security, identity, and self. For Jews, that sense of living with contradictions extends back to our earliest beginnings. A small people, we spread our poetry and prayers around the world. A weak people, we articulated notions of good and evil that have challenged and restrained the most powerful nations of the world. Our own age is not free of contradictions and ambiguities, either. As we rejoice in the rich cultural and religious life of so many contemporaries, we simultaneously worry about the threatening blandishments of assimilation, materialism, and indifference.

There is a time for everything under the heavens. Our struggle is that we have everything under the heavens all at once. To ignore the real accomplishments of democracy, reason, and spirituality would be to impugn the power of the human soul, the triumph of a worthy vision to establish itself and to contribute to the development of a more humane and caring world.

Yet to focus only on our achievements would be Pollyannaish—a superficial ignorance of the risk that ours may be the last generation, that our cultures, our religions, and our humanity face severe threats to our survival and our health.

As did our ancestors, we must learn to live with paradox. Survival may be in question, but our attitudes toward life play an essential role in determining our future. If we only fret over our losses, we will miss the opportunity to muster our resources for the fight ahead. If, on the other hand, we espouse a facile optimism—asserting that all is well and ignoring serious challenges—we may not see the need to mobilize. And there is a need to mobilize.

Judaism has always been a religion that insists on confronting reality directly. The best of secular culture, with its lofty humanism and its embrace of scientific method, starts with an embrace of realism. Death, suffering, and evil remain significant realities that our approach to life refuses to deny or minimize. The Reality Principle— that we must recognize reality as life's starting point—has guided our path from Judaism's inception.

But so has a stubborn refusal to despair. Humans have had ample reason to succumb to debilitating grief—millennia of persecution, bigotry, the perversion of religious power and forced conversion, and over a century of mindless hostility to liberation movements and national self-expression. Yet humanity as a whole never despaired. Instead, our confidence in our future, our love of Scripture, tradition, and good deeds, of learning and of family, carried us through the centuries.

Our challenge has always been to recognize reality as it is, while simultaneously working to transform reality into what it ought to be.

The story of the binding of Isaac is a powerful precedent for sustaining our dual commitment, for recognizing the dangers of reality while still insisting that we shall overcome.

When you reexamine the biblical story, you see that paradoxes abound: in God commanding Abraham to sacrifice his son, yet promising that the covenant would continue through that same son; in the willingness of both Abraham and Isaac to carry out God's shocking command, despite Abraham's vocal protest of God's intended destruction of Sodom and Gomorrah; in the complete absence of Sarah from the story despite her centrality in previous moments in Abraham's life.

Perhaps most puzzling of all is the very idea of God testing a chosen friend: "It was after these things, God tested Abraham" (Genesis 22:1). Indeed, Rabbinic tradition sees this test as the tenth and supreme trial God imposed on Abraham, "Our father Abraham was tested with ten trials and he withstood them all. This demonstrates our father Abraham's great love for God" (Pirkei Avot 5:4).

But what, precisely, is this test about?

Is the test whether or not Abraham would engage in child sacrifice? We know that human sacrifice was widespread in antiquity. Cemeteries with the remains of sacrificed children, and even an example of a pagan king who sacrificed his son within the Tanakh itself, testify to the far-too-frequent perception that the gods require human offerings. If that is so, then Abraham would not have been surprised that his God, like everybody else's, demanded a child sacrifice. Noting that his God is more like other deities than he had previously surmised, Abraham would have simply recognized this demand as being typical of what Supreme Beings generally require.

So if human sacrifice is not the test, if the suspension of the ethical is not unusual, then what is it that Abraham is being tested on?

## Living with Paradox

Abraham's trial, I would suggest, is his ability to live with paradox, to be able to take the tension inherent in human existence and use that tension to generate growth, insight, and depth. Tension can be fruitful; its resolution can lead to a higher plateau. The paradox that faces Abraham challenges us as well today. In the face of an ominous and threatening reality, how can we affirm our trust in God's promise to the Jewish people? In other words, how can we act with sufficient confidence and commitment to ensure that the best of our traditions and faith survive and grow? How can we contribute to a reality that adheres more closely to our highest ideals?

If we look back in the Bible, we see that just one chapter earlier, God had assured Abraham, "It is through Isaac that offspring shall be continued for you" (Genesis 21:12).

God promises Abraham that the *brit*, the covenant, made between Abraham and God, a covenant that extends to the children of Abraham throughout time, will be transmitted through Isaac. And then, one short chapter later, God orders Abraham to sacrifice that same son, thereby threatening the promise of a Jewish future.

Abraham's test, in short, is to live with that paradox: to hold onto the polar opposites of the world as it is and the world as it might be, refusing to abandon either one in the process of repairing them both. Abraham's test is to accept God's command to go through the motions of offering up Isaac, fully confident that Isaac would indeed be the vehicle through which the covenant with his heirs would begin.

Indeed, we see hints of that insight throughout the story. Whereas Abraham always spoke out against injustice in the past, in this moment—most crucial of all!—he is silent. How to explain his silence except to recognize the boundless depth of his faith that the crisis was only apparent, that his God would not abandon his covenant with the Jews?

Or, again, the silence is broken only once, in a conversation between father and son that marks their only recorded conversation in the entire Torah! Isaac asks his father, "Here is the flame and the wood; but where is the sheep for the burnt offering?" (Genesis 22:7).

Abraham's response shows us how to make sense out of this story. His reply is traditionally translated as "God will see to the sheep for [God's] burnt offering, my son" (22:8). Yet I must tell you that the punctuation of the biblical text is medieval and might be more profitably read in a different way. Following contemporary spiritual leader Rabbi Sheldon Zimmerman, we can also hear Abraham as saying, "God will see. He has the lamb for the offering, my son."

In that second reading, Abraham reveals to his pliable son that the lamb for the offering will be on the top of the mountain when they get there. Abraham's faith is that strong.

And, in fact, Abraham proves to be right. Once Isaac is strapped to the altar, they do find a ram trapped in the branches of a nearby tree. God does provide the offering on the mountaintop. But what of the first part of Abraham's response, where he claims, "God will see"?

These words are so significant that when Abraham names the altar where his son is to be sacrificed, he calls it "God will see."

What is it that Abraham knew God would see? And what is it that God will see in our lifetimes?

What God sees on that mountaintop is that Abraham and Isaac are there—body, mind, and soul. When God calls them, no matter how paradoxical is the call, those two respond actively, totally. To God's summons, they both say, "*Hineni*—Here I am."

Abraham does not deny the terror of his situation. He does not ignore the pain and the uncertainty of what he is ordered to do. But he refuses to surrender to the pain and the fear. He refuses to allow the situation to undermine his identity as a Jew.

Abraham's test is whether, in trying times, he will still insist on his core identity, still retain confidence that God's promised covenant will survive. By refusing to abandon hope in the face of a bleak reality, by refusing to wish away a challenging reality in favor of simplistic beliefs and wishful stories, Abraham remains true to the *brit*, the covenant.

We, too, face that same test. In the luxurious abundance of the West, in a world assaulted by terror, poverty, illness, and bigotry, we are called to recognize the reality of the threats facing us, to admit the statistical improbability of survival, and then to do the hard work necessary to transcend those statistics.

We, like Abraham, are tested with paradox.

For we, too, are the heirs to the promise, and the transmitters of that promise. God needs us to supply the hands to do the work, the hearts to bear the love, the mouths to give voice to the ancient primal utterance.

Like Abraham and Isaac before us, we, too, can say, "*Hineni*—we are here."

With faith in the merit and permanence of spiritual resurgence, recognizing that the reality of our lives and our community require special effort on our part, we, too, can pass the test.

*Hineni.*

# Priorities

## Balancing Spontaneity and Foresight

What, we may ask, is life all about? Is life just the meaningless eruption between an eternal darkness before birth and an empty nothingness after death? Or is there purpose to our time on earth, some large and beautiful plan that lends significance to our days and deeds?

Whether we choose it or not, whether we like it or not, each one of us is occupied with the business of living. Presented with twenty-four hours each day and seven days each week, the time is ours; we must account for it somehow.

Most of the time, that process is not one that involves a great deal of contemplation—there are jobs that need completion, chores that require attention, and people who expect our assistance. So we spend our days doing what we must. We are generally so busy with our daily routines that there is little time remaining to stop and ask ourselves larger questions about why we do what we do. What is the goal of all this busyness? Is there a reason to stay alive or is life simply a brute reality to which we submit without purpose?

Often we can live without the need for a reason to live. There are moments, however, when we are not graced with such tranquility. Instead, we find our nights assaulted by awareness of our own frailty and life's finitude. Odd and inconvenient questions—Why am I alive? What is the point of living? Who will remember me when I'm gone? Why care at all?—pop into our thoughts uninvited, chasing us through the corridors of our tumult, invading the privacy of our quiet and solitude.

No one can avoid such questions forever. The Greek philosopher Socrates taught that life teaches us the art of relinquishing. We learn to relinquish our own youth, we raise children who will live lives no longer centered around us, we watch helplessly as the people who raised us grow older and weaker. We face financial difficulties, competition, and disappointment. Of necessity, we learn to say good-bye as friends move away, as loved ones pass on. And someday, we anticipate with dread, we will have to say good-bye to life itself.

Human beings are the only creatures who must endure the possession of such unwelcome knowledge. We live under the tyranny of time—the awareness that we have only a limited amount of it and that the quality of the remaining days eludes both our control and our prediction.

We live in a world that is often chaotic, in which our most sublime hopes are made ridiculous and our most cherished connections are inevitably sundered. We live under the shadow of that reality—the awareness of what the world is like—even when times are good.

The central challenge confronting all of us, all humanity, is how to live in the face of incoherence and chaos. What is good? What does God require of us? How can we fashion meaning and community when our lives are in the grip of absurdity and happenstance?

The world has no shame. At funerals, I've often felt embarrassed as we bury the remains of a lovely and caring human being while the sun still shines, the birds still fly, and the voices of children at play waft from beyond the confines of the cemetery. As a rabbi, I have literally driven from a baby-naming celebration to a funeral to a wedding.

How dare the world go on? How can we stand to dance, knowing that in the midst of our community, friends and family are wrestling with unspeakable loss or limitless fear?

Yet we do go on, and life does continue. We are held in the indifferent pincers of time and human nature, unable to wriggle free.

"It was not your will that formed you, nor was it your will that gave you birth; it is not your will that makes you live, and it is not your will that brings you death" (Pirkei Avot 4:29). We are trapped on a roller coaster that will not stop and will not shift its course.

Knowing all that, how can we go on living? How can we make meaning and shelter for each other and ourselves in the world as it really is?

For the spiritual person, the central arena in the struggle of life is not just the world. Society can change slowly, and individuals gradually acquire new insight. But the pain and senselessness of aging, illness, and death are eternal. All humanity is locked into the vise of time. As it moves, we age, advance, let go. The world does not change; we do.

Which means, as I indicated already, that the primary arena of response to the reality of the world is in the human heart, the human soul. How we respond to the world can spell the difference between hope and meaning on the one hand, and despair and irrelevance on the other. How *we* respond.

## Present versus Future

Human nature offers two modes of response, two ways to overcome the paralyzing grip of time and its passing. In the words of Rabbi Judah ha-Nasi, "Some attain eternity over several years, while others do so in an instant" (Talmud, Avodah Zarah 10b).

To "attain eternity over several years": This first response to the passing of time and its randomness is to immerse ourselves in the patient unfolding of a way of life. Rather than expending our energy on the present—which in any case is over in a flash—this approach sees the present as the opportunity to invest in a better tomorrow. By cultivating the path of study, discipline, and activism, we hope to create a future of transforming value.

To attain eternity "in an instant": This second method is a struggle to transcend the passing of time, to live for the present, to revel in the moment. Such an approach insists that the past is over and done with; the future is unreliable. All we have and all we really are is in the present. Therefore, this moment—now—must be fashioned into a moment of such purity and perfection that it will epitomize our values; it will crystallize as a memorial for all time to come.

Both approaches address a similar problem: the tragic absurdity of life. Both possess considerable advantages and weaknesses. Living in the moment or preparing for the future—both responses seek to overcome the limits of human impotence, chaos, and death.

We meet those two approaches in the first two leaders of the Hebrews, in our patriarchs Abraham and Isaac.

Abraham is the archetypal planner, always living for the future, always building a better tomorrow. He is the wanderer, leaving the known in favor of a tomorrow in a place as yet undetermined. We meet Abraham when God commands him to break with the past, to "Go forth ... to the land that I will show you" (Genesis 12:1). God's first words to Abraham speak of his distant descendants: "I will make of you a great nation" (Genesis 12:2). His very introduction is one directed toward the yet to come.

At the age of seventy-five, Abraham and his wife, Sarah, venture off to a new land, to Canaan. There, he immediately puts himself into the stream of history, the connection of one point in time with all future points. He purchases land and builds altars—both of these deeds presume a return at some later date. He wages war with five kings, and he signs a contract with local chieftains. In all things, Abraham is a statesman and a diplomat, a man who plans today for the tomorrow he hopes to build. Abraham is the visionary, the dreamer.

Not so his son, Isaac. Isaac lives for today. We meet Isaac in the very thickness of the present, as two women struggle for the right to raise their sons. Hagar and Sarah fight for now, knowing that life now is all there really is. Abraham remains somewhat distant; he doesn't value today, so he leaves it to the women to dispute. Isaac learns from his mother.

Abraham's birth is barely mentioned; what matters about Abraham isn't a single moment of the present, but the stream of moments leading to the future. Isaac's birth, however, is heralded by an angelic visit. For him, throughout his life, it is the present moment that lives and shines. "This is the day the LORD has made! Let us exult and rejoice on it" (Psalm 118:24).

While Abraham engages in public statecraft, we hear nothing of Isaac, whose profoundly private life bears no public import. While Abraham is planning and shaping, Isaac's energy is absorbed by being.

## Transcending Time's Grip

Father and son on separate paths, both wrestling with life's absurdity, both choosing very different ways to transcend time's grip.

Then, according to contemporary Bible scholar Professor Aharon Agus, eternity and the present, the path and the moment, come together in one stunning occasion: the trial of Abraham, the binding of Isaac.

The Bible tells us that "God tested Abraham" (Genesis 22:1). God commands Abraham, the great planner, the man who lives today so that the covenant can flourish tomorrow, that he must sacrifice his very son, the embodiment of all tomorrows yet to come. Abraham's trial is to learn to live in the present, to value today regardless of tomorrow.

For Abraham, then, the trial is to stop being the planner, to live fully in the present. His son no longer represents a glorious future. Isaac will live only a few more days. The test for Abraham is to live without dreams, to love without plans.

The Torah tells us that Abraham passes the test. In the two days that father and son spend walking together toward Mount Moriah, Abraham learns that simply being together in the present can forge an eternity of meaning and love. The two do not exchange more than two sentences the entire time, and those are of a technical nature. Rather than planning for the future, Abraham is forced to simply savor his son's presence and his son's present. Ultimately, that is all there is.

And Isaac? What is his test?

Simple arithmetic calculations show that at the time that God made this demand on his father, Isaac was a strapping man of 37 years. His father was well over 140. There is no way that the aged Abraham could have bound his adult son to the altar to be slain if Isaac did not actively participate in the event.

Remember, Isaac lives for the moment. Recognizing the chaos and disappointment inherent in life, Isaac sees his only avenue of escape as creating one staggering moment of purpose—a purpose so transcendent, so stunning, that it lends eternal meaning to any subsequent memory. Isaac sees this moment, the binding, as his moment, his chance to soar above the reality of passing time, to select his own way of defining his life's purpose.

Perhaps, then, Isaac's test is that God doesn't allow the sacrifice to take place. Rather than becoming a martyr, Isaac is forced to enter the stream of history, to become a part of the ongoing march of the Jewish people through time, to use the *mitzvot*, sacred deeds, to infuse his life with holiness. Instead of one blinding moment of glory, Isaac must train himself to make his routine a steady progression of redemption and meaning.

The Rabbis of the Midrash note that at the end of the binding incident the Bible states, "Abraham returned" (Genesis 22:19). Where, they ask, is Isaac? Rabbi Berekiah said, "Abraham sent him to the Academy of Shem to learn the Torah" (*Bereshit Rabbah* 56:19). In other words, after retreating from the brink of martyrdom, with the drama and glory of a martyr's death, Isaac must take up the far more difficult task of sanctifying the mundane, of bringing God's healing presence to everyday living.

Abraham, the planner, learns that he must become open to the power of the moment. Isaac, the spontaneous one, learns that he must plan and build. Both, it seems, were tested, and both learned something.

There is a place for the moment, for living in the present. Far too often we fail to value what is truly ours, longing instead for some future perfection. Rabbi Pesach Krauss, the chaplain of Memorial Sloan-Kettering Cancer Center in Manhattan, writes in his poignant memoirs, *Why Me? Coping with Grief, Loss and Change*:

> How priceless are those simple things—sunlight, a moment, a touch, family, friends, love. And how careless we are of our most valued treasures. We take them for granted, as if they are coming to us. As if we could hold on to them forever.

In the horror of the binding, Abraham learns not to take his son for granted. Isaac is not merely the next step in a sacred plan; he is a living human being, of infinite value for his own sake, not for his usefulness. Abraham learns to cherish those he loves, to make time for them now. Immediately after the binding, Abraham occupies himself with more human and fatherly tasks—finding a wife for his son, spending energy on his family and his home.

We, too, squander our finite time planning for a day that may never come. Are you saving so you can spend time with your family after you retire? Spend that time now, while you have your health and your family. Are you out of touch with a child, a parent, or a dear friend because of some long-ago fight? Make a move to repair that breach. If you already tried, try again. Have you wanted to grow spiritually and emotionally, to put more time into your faith? Don't put that off. "Do not say, 'When I have leisure, I will study,' for you may never have leisure" (Pirkei Avot 2:5).

As tempting as it is to live only for today, tomorrow will come, and there are people who depend on our preparations today to be able to enjoy their tomorrows. If we aren't willing to invest our time in acquiring useful skills, we won't be able to support our families and ourselves in the future. If we don't learn the sacred texts of our tradition, who will be able to read them for our grandchildren? If we don't translate the rhythms of holy days and festivals into the flow of our lives, then who will build those precious memories for the seekers yet to come? If we don't visit the sick, feed the hungry, or help advance justice and peace, then who will be there to visit or to comfort us? If we don't work today to clean our skies and purify our water, we won't be able to bequeath a livable world to our children. If we don't insist on a world order that prohibits acts of aggression and bans nuclear weapons, then we may literally obliterate the hopes for the tomorrows that might have been.

The world needs our preparation. Elie Wiesel, upon receiving the Nobel Prize in 1986, remarked in his acceptance speech, "We know that every moment is a moment of grace, every hour an offering." His words echo the gratitude of our ancient prayer to God: "In Your goodness, day after day You renew Creation."

How do we balance the piercing intensity of the present with the persistent call of the future? By returning to the earliest mission of our ancient ways, by returning to God. For, ultimately, eternity and the present meet in the loving heart of God. The Holy Ancient One who always was and will always be, the Fount of life and hope of humanity, is the One for whom present, past, and future coexist. By making ourselves known to God, by cultivating gratitude and holiness that can pervade every aspect of our lives—how we work, how we live, and how we play—we fuse the eternal and the instant.

Abraham faces that test. Isaac faces that test. And we, too, are tested today. Live today; prepare for a better tomorrow.

# Solidarity

## Of Love and Loyalties

The English poet William Shakespeare claims, "Love is not love which alters when it alteration finds" (Sonnet 116). In other words, real love never changes, never retreats, and never surrenders.

That lovely ideal might be true were we to love one person at a time, thus avoiding any competition for our attention or our resources. But most of us juggle an assortment of simultaneous relationships—lover or spouse, children, parents, friends, synagogue, God, nation, and planet. Rare is the person who is only called on to love once. Instead, we allocate our limited time and energy to satisfy as many needs of these competing relationships as our strength and our love will permit.

It is an unavoidable reality of human life that the many roles one person plays in a single lifetime—that of child, parent, lover, friend, citizen, and seeker—all take time, require effort, and deserve more than a person can possibly devote to any one of them. With the best of intentions, we are doomed to disappoint ourselves, destined to juggle our multiple commitments of love forever.

It would be easy if the choice were between those we love and those we do not. Then, in fact, there would be no choice at all. But far too often we are forced to choose between two laudable loves: the mother whose infant cries just as her husband complains that they never talk; the adult son whose widowed mother belittles his wife at every visit; the harried father with too little time at home and too little money for the family, forced to choose one or the other, doomed to feel inadequate regardless of which path he chooses. Children often feel torn between their desire to be with their friends and the demands of their parents for more time as a family.

On and on, the really difficult issues in life involve conflicting loves. It would be easy if it were just "you and me against the world." But it is rarely that simple. Instead, our already busy lives and strapped budgets become the battleground between insecure relatives, insistent friends, and our own desire to be with the people we love.

We are not the first to face this conflict. Out of the pain and darkness of the story of Abraham's trial and Isaac's binding emerge wise counsel for responding to the human needs and desires of those we love, as well as a healthy restraint on the demands we impose on each other and ourselves.

## Loves Lost, Loves Affirmed

Abraham is a devoted man of God. Time and time again the Torah celebrates his commitment to the Creator of the Universe, so that Abraham's soul embraces God's requests with an unquestioning "Here I am" (Genesis 22:1). Leaving his childhood home, Abraham has already faced the conflict between loyalty to parents and commitment to a cause. Undeterred in his love for God, he gathers his immediate family and leaves the idolatrous place of his youth, wandering across the expanse of what is now Iraq, Iran, Syria, and Jordan to his destination in the Land of Israel. There he and his beloved Sarah serve God faithfully, rewarded with a bustling household, robust health, and growing wealth.

The one thing that Abraham doesn't have is a child. Like any other Hebrew, Abraham knows that a child is the supreme blessing. A pious and devoted man, he petitions God throughout his long life. Finally, at the ripe age of one hundred, Abraham becomes the happy father to Isaac, who—God assures him—will be Abraham's heir and his link to a nation that will elevate the standard for human spirituality and ethics.

Isaac is the crown of his father's life, infusing Abraham's existence with both meaning and companionship. Delighted by Isaac's birth, Abraham responds to his son's needs with that same spontaneous "Here I am" (Genesis 22:7) that the devoted father had offered to God.

Abraham's life is now complete. Obedient servant to the one true God, caring father of a beautiful child, healthy and rich, what else could Abraham need? In his blessed life, the love of his God and of his son intertwine, each resonating to a single harmony, each fortifying the other.

Then, late one evening, God shatters Abraham's sleep, destroying his tranquility forever:

> Please take your son, your favored, whom you love, Isaac, and go to the land of Moriah, and offer him there as an offering on one of the mountains that I will tell you. (Genesis 22:2)

That endless night must have felt like an eternity. Deliberately putting Abraham's love to the test, God requires that he sacrifice the most precious relationship he knows: his future, his fulfillment, his son.

Imagine Abraham's agony in the still of that miserable night. The choice before him is either to betray his God, the source of his blessing and the root of his integrity, or to slaughter his son! Love conflicts with love in a way that admits no escape, no fudging. As the light of dawn illuminates the gray-pink sky, Abraham knows he has to choose between loyalties. There is no way out.

The Torah records that he makes a decision, although the choice is far from easy. Abraham first tries to placate God by pretending not to understand. The Midrash describes a painful conversation between the reluctant Abraham and his insistent God:

> God said, "*Take your son.*" "Which son?" Abraham asked. "*Your only son,*" replied God. "But each is the only son of his mother," said Abraham. "*Whom you love,*" replied God. "Is there a limit to my affections?" said Abraham. "*Isaac,*" insisted God. (*Bereshit Rabbah* 55:7)

Rising early in the morning, rousing his sleepy son and his tired servants, Abraham himself saddles his donkey and collects the wood for the sacrifice. In itself, that deviation from protocol must have raised eyebrows: Why would the wealthy and venerable patriarch stoop to such manual labor? Why not summon servants to do that strenuous work? Yet our ancient Rabbis understood: this was to be a personal test of his love. In the words of Rabbi Shimon bar Yohai, "Love obliterates all normal standards" (*Bereshit Rabbah* 55:8).

That challenge of conflicting loyalty is not Abraham's alone. At the same time, Isaac, after all, is thirty-seven years old. He's healthy, strong, and easily able to overpower his elderly father. No divine words are addressed to him, and the fullness of life still pulses through his veins. Caught between the demands of filial reverence, religious obedience, and the mandate to live, Isaac, too, stares down the chasm of irreconcilable commitments. It is clear that Isaac recognizes the conflict between God and Abraham, between his own binding and continued life. As *Avot de-Rabbi Natan* intuits, "While Isaac agreed with his mouth, he said in his heart, 'Who will save me from my father? I have no help except from the Holy One.'" Yet, despite the conflict, Isaac casts his lot with his father. The Torah records, "And the two walked together" (Genesis 22:8), which the ancient commentary *Pseudo-Yonatan* clarifies as, "They went together with a whole heart."

Once having committed himself, Isaac's solidarity with God and Abraham is unshakable. Along the way, after Isaac discovers the chilling truth of his future, he still responds, "My soul is bound up with God and with my father. Anything he [He?] wants to do, he [He?] will do" (*Midrash Va-Yosha* 36).

Yet the bravado of father and son, united in their loyalty to God, is poignantly tragic, marred by the betrayal and violence that shadow their purpose. One obscure midrash hints at this agony—the tug of their dual allegiance. Even as Isaac is bound on the altar, his father holding the knife above him,

God sat on the Throne of Glory and saw how their hearts were one, and the tears of Abraham rolled down and fell onto Isaac, and from Isaac they fell onto the wood of the altar, so it was submerged in their tears. (*Midrash Va-Yosha* 37)

The central question of the *Akedah*, then, is neither child sacrifice nor Abraham's faith. The central question facing both Abraham and Isaac is that of conflicting love, of competing loyalties. There is no way for them to reconcile their love for life, their love for each other, and their love for God. Something has to give.

That same question confronts every one of us, now and every day of our lives. How do we handle the tests of love that fill our lives with worry and strain? Many of those tests are unavoidable, painful moments that test our mettle and reveal our worth: Will *we* be there when *we* are needed? Will we be able to say "*Hineni*" when called by a child, a spouse, or a friend? Will we be able to respond, "Here I am" to the needs of the congregation, the community, or the timeless teachings of our faith?

With too little leisure and far too many needs to satisfy, can we better apportion our limited resources—time, energy, money—to meet the priorities and concerns of the significant people and causes in our lives?

## Competing Loyalties

Abraham and Isaac are tested by competing loyalties. They rise to the occasion of their test by facing their conflict head-on, by discussing what they have to do, and resolving jointly on a course of action. Perhaps the first lesson of the binding is that when a test comes our way, we need to discuss possible responses with the other parties affected by our choices.

The most important transformation in the binding, however, is not that of Abraham or that of Isaac. It is the transformation of God. God is the one who grows the most, teaching us through example, here as elsewhere.

At the outset, God sees the devotion of Abraham as compromised by a new competitor for love—Isaac. How better to test whether Abraham really loves God than to demand exclusive devotion? Construing love as a test, God insists on proof of Abraham's loyalty. The command "Sacrifice your son" emerges from an insecurity that seeks reassurance by requiring a test. For God, as for people, deliberately creating a test for love can only result in distress and, generally, also in failure.

The suffering of Abraham and Isaac, even as they willingly undergo God's imposed test, becomes too painful for God to bear. Even in winning, God loses. So God retreats from the original demand, calling out, "Do not send your hand against the lad" (Genesis 22:12). Remarkably, God admits to having learned something from this terrible test: "For now I know you fear God" (Genesis 22:12), or in Rashi's explanation to that same verse, "Henceforth I have an answer about My love toward you."

What is God's new answer? What does God know "now" that was mystifying before this test?

I propose that God learns not to test love. God retreats from the demand of full or exclusive devotion, stops insisting on rights or prerogatives. Instead, God recognizes that we each do the best we can, balancing busy schedules, multiple relationships, and many separate commitments. Rather than comparing, God learns to admire the depth of those different loves. God never poses such a test again.

## A Revolution of Vision

Ultimately, this test of Abraham is a revolution of vision. God no longer construes loyalty in terms of competition and opposition, moving instead to a fuller vision of harmony and complementarity. Our roles as child, parent, spouse, friend, Jew, and American need not always conflict. By refusing to pose tests, lines in the sand that we dare each other to pass or to fail, we can, like God in the binding, learn to spare each other and ourselves great strife and sorrow.

Instead of competing for love and commitment, instead of pitting loyalty against loyalty, can we not admit that love and loyalty ought, in the words of philosopher Josiah Royce, in *The Philosophy of Loyalty*,

> to unify life, to give it center, fixity, stability? One should choose a
> cause that will further, rather than frustrate, the loyalties of others,
> as well as one's own multiple loyalties. (p. 22)

In other words, we express love and loyalty when we support the ability of each other to do the same, when we willingly offer what is morally demanded by the object of our love or commitment.

God learns, in short, that there are limits to what one can demand of others, no matter how close they may be. Abraham and Isaac learn that love cannot survive a deliberate test, that something precious will always be killed in the process. And together they learn to say a more moderate "Here I am" only to what is moral, only to what is possible, knowing in advance that we cannot be all things to all people, even to ourselves.

Paradoxically, by accepting our own limitations, we free ourselves from the burdens of limitless expectations and consequent disappointment. Able to meet reasonable needs and to share love in specific intervals, we move from *nisayon* as "test" to *nisayon* as "experience." No longer an artificial exercise doomed to fail, these experiences, like a string of pearls, can each add luster and beauty to the texture of our lives.

# Faith, Fear, and Faithfulness

## Can Faith Save?

One of the central dilemmas challenging many modern men and women, and certainly many modern Jews, is that we turn for comfort and purpose to a faith whose tenets we often find too simplistic or downright unacceptable. Even as we affirm the importance of being faithful, even as we struggle to support religious education and to transmit ancient identity, we harbor our own doubts, not just about the peripheral details of religious life, but about the very core of our ancestral faith. How can we believe in a Creation of the world when we have seen the overwhelming and meticulous evidence for a Big Bang and for evolution? How can we affirm a God who intervenes and saves only after six million have been murdered by the Nazis or after the brutal destruction of hurricanes and tsunamis? How can we affirm a loving God in a world with SIDS, AIDS, cancer, and so much debilitating suffering?

In our suffering, we still seek solace. In our disappointment, we still need hope. So we dance a mental two-step, hopping between the pious sentiments of our ancient sacred texts and prayer books, while living and thinking like every other contemporary. Our sacred texts remain hermetically sealed, incapable of withstanding the realities of skepticism, sophistication, and modernity. Or so we fear. So in an attempt to protect our heritage from the harsh blasts of reality, and to preserve our traditions at least as a lovely bauble to admire and to cherish, we keep them closed off from our daily lives.

Our traditions may remain sealed, but they remain nonetheless. Most of us are unwilling to turn over our lives to them entirely, but we are equally unwilling to jettison them forever. Unable to wholeheartedly embrace the core convictions of faith and equally unwilling to walk away from them, we are chained to traditions that cannot hold us, and we risk the paralysis of indecision and emptiness. Small wonder that so many look elsewhere for spiritual nurture. Small wonder that so many associate their heritage with traditions and with festivals rather than with spiritual depth and profound wisdom.

Is there a way out of this dilemma? Is there room for faith following the bloody and disappointing twentieth century? Or must faith and spirit go the way of the horse and buggy, a charming relic of a simpler age? How can a sophisticated modern person believe?

## Wrestling with Reality versus Our Ideals

While we like to imagine that our problems are unique to our own time, I am convinced that we are not the first generation to wrestle with the chasm that separates our hopes from our reality, our dreams from our daily lives. Perhaps it is the arrogance of each generation to consider itself unprecedented. Perhaps that is what thirteenth-century philosopher Moses Maimonides was referring to when he asserted that the purpose of the ram's horn (shofar) is to "rouse those who sleep in the bonds of time" (*Mishneh Torah*, Laws of Repentance 3:4), those of us trapped by the arrogance of the present. The truth is that we are not the first to see an unbridgeable gap between what is and what ought to be, and we are not the first to confront experiences that test our essence and sear our faith.

In wrestling with the rift between reality and our ideals, our sacred traditions can provide an essential tool for navigating these tumultuous times. It is the glory of our ancient literature to confront these challenges, honestly and openly, without imposing superficial answers or rigid dogma to mask the pain of not knowing and the anguish of not being able to make it all right.

Perhaps that honesty is modernity's greatest gift to faith: its remarkable ability to assure its children that there are questions worth asking even when the answers elude us, even when there may never be any final answers within human grasp. Surely the questions of life and death, suffering and reward, our place in the cosmos, our obligations to our fellow human beings and to all living things are among those that human beings have flung to heaven as much in accusation as out of a desire to hear an explanation. Those burning arrows disguised as theology still torment the hearts of parents who suffer over a child's illness, spouses who helplessly watch their soul mates eaten away by disease, and all caring people who suffer the callousness and brutality of some of their fellow human beings.

In light of these unanswerable questions, queries spring from deep within and faith shines ever brighter because of its wisdom in framing essential issues without imposing a smug, self-satisfied, and ultimately shallow answer.

Through story, deed, and law, spiritual traditions teach us that what really matters in such questions aren't the questions at all, and certainly not the scripted answers that so often leave us feeling hollow and unsatisfied. What matters in such things is the attitude of the person who is asking the question. What matters is an orientation of faithfulness and trust.

## Faith and Faithfulness

There is no better biblical example of trusting faithfulness than Abraham and the binding of Isaac. Perhaps because the Rabbis of the Talmud recognized the difficulty of maintaining faith (*emunah*) even in their own day, they selected this Torah portion for the second day of Rosh Ha-Shanah. Perhaps they recognized that we could all learn from Abraham, from considering how his faith helped him in his trial, and by recognizing what his faith could not do.

Recall that Abraham already has a reputation as a beloved and faithful servant of God. Years before the binding of Isaac, God had already assured Abraham of security and well-being:

Fear not, Abram,

I am a shield to you;

Your reward shall be very great! (Genesis 15:1)

With good reason, then, Abraham expects a life of relative ease and comfort. In recognition that with wealth and status comes responsibility, Abraham spends his life working for the betterment of humanity and for more adherents to the one true God. He and his wife, Sarah, indeed grow wealthy, returning from their stay in Egypt as the prosperous heads of a booming household and a growing tribe of people. But for the lack of a child, their lives are complete.

Even with the expectation of progeny, Abraham has the comfort of divine assurance. After all, God had already told him, "Look toward the heaven and count the stars.... So shall your offspring be" (Genesis 15:5).

Sure enough, that promise is fulfilled, along with all the others. Prior to Isaac's birth, Abraham and Sarah are told, "You shall name him Isaac; and I will maintain My covenant with him as an everlasting covenant" (Genesis 17:19).

Imagine their thrill at finally having a son, someone to love and to hold, and someone to continue the religious and moral traditions that the prominent father and the energetic mother have initiated so recently. Isaac is to be their greatest blessing.

Then comes that fateful day. Out of the blue, we are told, "God tested Abraham" (Genesis 22:1). And what is the nature of this test? Abraham is to be the instrument of his son's death. Not only is the poor father to bind his son to the altar, he is to be the one to sacrifice his beloved Isaac.

Can you imagine a greater crisis, a greater test of faithfulness than what Abraham had to endure? Loving his son more than life itself, having devoted his life to the service of God, Abraham now is in precisely the position of so many moderns, having to choose, apparently, between his firmest dreams of how life ought to be and how it is unfolding, relentlessly, before him. How is Abraham to cope? Can his faith help him at all? Can faith help us?

## A Personal *Akedah*

There was an occasion when I found myself thinking of Abraham and the *Akedah*. After twenty-six weeks of a difficult pregnancy with twins, Elana, my wife, had to be rushed to the hospital in a desperate attempt to stop premature contractions that could have led to delivery. I don't need to point out that babies at twenty-six weeks of gestation are in mortal danger, due to their lack of development. Full term, for those who still think in terms of months, is forty weeks. At twenty-six weeks, our babies, if they were born, would not have had a good chance of survival.

Elana and I drove to the hospital, accompanied by dear friends. The nurses put Elana in a hospital bed and injected her with a drug that relaxes the uterus. As we waited for her contractions to stop, Elana's physiology took a different course. She began to sweat heavily, her eyes rolled back, and she passed out before our eyes. As the nurses worked feverishly to bring her back to consciousness, they noticed that the heartbeat of one of the twins—the boy—was fluctuating wildly, seriously endangering the baby.

That was when the crisis began in earnest. Nurses and doctors appeared, as if from thin air. Shouts of "Prep the OR" were my only clue that Elana was about to be rushed into the operating room, that life and death hung in the balance. I recall that a nurse pushed me out the door and told me to wait, and when I next saw Elana, she was strapped to a portable bed, while nurses were running her into the operating room. I realized that they were going to do an emergency C-section—at twenty-six weeks!

I ran after my beloved wife, thinking all the while, "It's not supposed to be this way! It's not supposed to be this way!" As Elana disappeared behind the doors of the operating room, one kind nurse gave me surgical scrubs to dress in and then told me to wait. I sat on a plastic chair in the hallway, alone in the world, as nurses and doctors ran in and out of the surgical suite. I didn't know whether or not the operation had begun, and no one had any spare time to keep me informed. Elana and I had not had a chance to speak to each other since we entered the hospital a few hours earlier.

I rocked back and forth on that chair, and I paced up and down the hallway. All the while, I was talking to God and crying. I pleaded with God on behalf of our babies, "Dear God, they are so little, so innocent. Please let them live." Even as I spoke, I knew that God doesn't pull strings in the universe, doesn't cause cancer for some and assure health for favored others. Such a God would be a monster, and such a God is certainly not in evidence in the world. Despite my conviction that God doesn't act in that way, I still had the need to pray. So I prayed.

And I prayed for Elana, my life. Lying on that table were all my ideals, my dreams, my future, and my identity. I would sooner have had them cut me than touch her.

Yet I also knew that, in some sense, we had chosen this path together. We had both decided that we wanted to raise children of our own, and we both knew the risks involved in having twins. We had made a choice to walk down this path, however excruciating our present condition was.

Finally, they allowed me into the OR. Elana, looking pale and shaking both from terror and from cold, was strapped onto the operating table. The doctors surrounding the table picked up the scalpels to cut my wife. Then their eyes fell on the screen of the monitor and, behold, the boy's heart rate had stabilized. As they saw this salvation from the side, they realized that they didn't have to raise a hand against Elana or do anything to her except to watch her for the night. As tensions eased, we realized that we had endured our own personal *Akedah*.

How had my faith helped me through that terrible night, an evening that I hope will be the worst night of my entire life? Was my faith a source of comfort to me? Was God there with us as we prepared to offer our most precious gifts to the knife?

I will tell you one thing that my faith didn't do, and that I didn't ask of it: the questions I hurled up to God were not meant as real questions. I was not operating in the mode of thought and analysis. That comes later, after the fact. My questions were really pleas, hopes, terror, and rage masquerading as prayer. While the surface may have been words and discourse, the actual core—what I was seeking in my fear and anguish—was beyond words. I was seeking belonging, rootedness, and connection.

Judaism provided that. In my deepest terror, I never felt alone. Even in my fear, I could sense the nurturing love of my community, the connection to the Jewish people, our rootedness in the *mitzvot*, and the love and concern of God. I didn't have answers, but I had *emunah*, the ability to trust in faithfulness.

How can I describe for you what eludes description? How can I point you to what *emunah* can mean? One time, when we had a series of earthquakes in California, my instinctive response was to remain in bed and relax. Somehow I would just float with it. As strange as that may sound, I trusted myself to the earthquake, even though in my mind I knew that I had no better guarantees than anybody else.

Once I was swimming in the ocean when a strong undertow started to pull me down. Again, my instinctive response was to go limp, trusting myself to the waves. As they dragged me down, slamming me against the sand at the bottom, I just let them pull me along, confident that those same waves would bring me to the surface again.

Faithfulness, *emunah*, felt exactly like going limp in the ocean or trusting myself to the earthquake. While we often mistake faith for mental assent to a list of verbal assertions ("I believe this, I believe that"), the Hebrew meaning of *emunah* isn't assent. It means "trust." To have faith is to be able to trust. To trust in something beyond ourselves, to trust that we have the strength and commitment to get through whatever comes; to trust that we are never alone.

Faith doesn't mean expecting to get a better deal because of our piety. It certainly doesn't mean expecting God to favor some people over other people as part of a bargain between a person and God. In fact, one understanding of the test of Abraham is precisely that Abraham was given that final trial in order to show that he wasn't trusting God in return for God taking care of him:

> God said, "I have tried you with many trials and you have passed them all successfully. Now, I beg you, for My sake, withstand this trial also, so that people will not say that all the earlier ones were without worth." (Talmud, Sanhedrin 82b)

Just as faith does not mean expecting the universe to treat us better than anyone else, so faith doesn't mean not having human fears, doubts, or feelings. Nowhere are we led to believe that Abraham isn't in bitter torment throughout the trial. His feelings as a father are powerful and conscious even while he gains some measure of comfort from his faith:

> And Abraham stretched forth his hand and took the knife to slay his son. He stretched forth his hand to take the knife, and tears fell from his eyes into the eyes of Isaac, because he felt the mercy of a father. But in spite of this he went joyfully to do the will of his Creator. (*Bereshit Rabbah* 46)

Faith, then, is not a matter of intellectual content or acumen; it is an attribute of trust, a sense of embeddedness and connection. Abraham is no philosopher, no logician. He doesn't stand by the altar posing complicated inquiries or balancing divergent theologies. He is an *ish emunah*, a person of faith, because he relies on his ability to trust even while beset by doubt, even when tortured by pain and loss.

We, too, face similar tests of faith and faithfulness all the time. Ancient tradition wisely observes, "There is no creature whom the Holy Blessing One does not test" (cited by Rabbi Sidney Greenberg). The great skill of the faithful is not that they can escape life's hurts, disappointments, and pains better than those who lack faith. The central gift of faith is simply the ability to view every encounter that comes to us as a test of our character and our integrity. When challenged by the suffering of those we love or of our own disappointments in life, *emunah* is the ability to retain the power of how we choose to respond and how we decide to act.

To be able to retain a sense of belonging to something transcendent and eternal, to know that we are a people in covenant with God and linked across generations one to another is a great source of strength and courage. It was with Abraham when he was tried by God; it was with Elana and me when our turn came. The ability to float, to turn over to God our need to control and manipulate, even while doing all we can to assist God in bringing about a positive outcome, is the very core of trusting faithfulness.

In that regard, the prayer of Rabbi Eliezer from the second century is still very much our own:

> *Do Your will, O God, in heaven above, and bestow tranquility*
> *of spirit on those who revere You below. And what is good in*
> *your sight, do. (Talmud, Berakhot 29b)*

# People above Principles

## And God Tested Sarah

*So far, all of our attention has focused on Abraham—the patriarch who is explicitly the subject of the biblical trial— and Isaac, the one on whom the sacrifice descends. But in all this testing and binding, the mother is left back at home, alone. There is no written record of any conversation to let her know what her husband was planning, or why he disappeared early one morning with her son. We read of no conversation between her and God, her and her husband, her and Isaac. Instead, she is shunted aside and silent. Can we peer through the lattice of the text to tease out a hidden tale and a subterranean insight? Perhaps the tools of midrash can create an opening for a little light.*

Sometime after Sarah's conflict with Hagar and Ishmael, and years focused on raising her son Isaac, God tested Sarah. God said to her, "Sarah," and she answered, "Here I am." And God said, "Please take your son, your favored, whom you love, Isaac, and go to the land of Moriah, and offer him there as an offering on one of the mountains that I will tell you."

And Sarah, who loved God for the miraculous gift of a son, was puzzled. She looked at God and said, "Who are You?"

God was confused. "What do you mean 'Who am I?' I am God, the Creator of the heavens and the earth, the one who molded Adam

79

from the earth and who breathed life into that first earthling. I am the One who caused Adam to sleep and then who split Adam into both man and woman. You know Me, Sarah. I've spoken to you before."

Sarah, still radiant in her old age, looked up to God and said, "No, You can't be that God. The God that I know is the God who tells us to choose life. The God that I know is the One who helps the barren have children and infuses the breath of life into all living things. That's the God I've learned to love. But a God who would have a mother kill her son must be someone else. So, again, I ask you: Who are You?"

God didn't know how to respond. Unwilling to give up so quickly, God made another stab at persuasion, this time trying the tack he would take with Job: "Were you there when I made the world? Can you tame Leviathan or overpower Behemoth? Can you silence the thunder or stop the rain? Who are you to question My ways?"

Unfazed, Sarah simply said, "Out of loyalty to the God I love, I will not do what You require. And You still haven't answered my question: Who are You?"

This time, God was stunned into silence. No one, after all, had ever spoken to God in this way. Not really knowing what to do, and uncertain that any approach would work with this determined but puzzling mother, God retreated, muttering something about not understanding women. After all, God's conversations with Eve had been just as puzzling: she had insisted on knowledge, regardless of the price!

Seeking familiar ground, God sought out Abraham. "Abraham," God called, and Abraham, who feared God for God's many signs of power, for whom service to God was the highest value, answered, "Here I am."

"Please take your son, your favored, whom you love, Isaac, and go to the land of Moriah, and offer him there as an offering on one of the mountains that I will tell you." Without hesitation, Abraham deferred to the divine decree. Early the next morning he saddled the donkey himself (that's how eager he was to do God's will). After waking Isaac and two servants, the men walked in silence toward Mount Moriah.

"Now that's more like it," thought God. Still, the Holy One couldn't silence the echo of Sarah's troubling question: "Who are You?" Turning it over and over, God was at a loss. After all, as the Source of everything, God was entitled to unquestioning obedience. Yet Sarah presented her refusal to obey God as an act of loyalty, not of rebellion!

"Women!" God muttered, although with a tremor of doubt in the thunderous voice. Still, at least Abraham was proving himself to be a resolute and unquestioning servant, which offered some measure of comfort.

Toward the beginning of the men's march toward Moriah, Isaac noticed a striking omission in his father's preparations.

"My father," said Isaac.

"Here I am, my son," answered Abraham.

"Here is the flame and the wood; but where is the sheep for the burnt offering?"

The aged patriarch looked at his son and could only answer, "God will see to the sheep for the offering, my son."

And the two of them walked on together.

After three days of silent togetherness, during which Abraham struggled to stifle the natural pity he felt as a father and to strengthen his sense of joy in fulfilling the will of his Creator, Abraham and his entourage finally made it to the mountaintop.

In silence, obedient to the divine decree, Abraham prepared the altar, placed the wood on it, bound his son Isaac, and laid him on the altar, on top of the wood. This was no small feat, since Isaac was nearly forty years old, at the full height of his powers. Isaac, too, however, sensed an opportunity to serve God by offering himself as the first martyr for the faith—a great honor indeed! So the younger man assisted the older man to the extent that someone bound could, and he lay as still as possible on the wood so his father could make a clean and kosher cut.

Relying on every bit of his fear of God, Abraham grasped the knife to slay his son and raised his hand high in the air.

And at that moment, God understood.

"Aha!" God exclaimed. "I know what she was asking me."

"Who am I? I am the God who delights in life, whose service constitutes choosing life. I can't ask my faithful to betray their commitment to life and to each other, since that's how they serve me most faithfully."

With a passion for life and for covenant renewed, God realized that Abraham would feel like a failure in his own eyes if God wasn't careful in how the test was called off. Yet somehow God had to teach Abraham to serve out of love, to transcend his fear of God with a more mature love of heaven. Meanwhile, Abraham's knife still gleamed in the air.

Without a second to waste, God called out to Abraham: "Abraham! Abraham!"

"Here I am," Abraham answered.

And God said, "Do not send your hand against the lad, and do nothing to him." Now came Abraham's test: could he grow from fear to love? Even while placing a substitute sacrifice in the nearby bush, God continued to speak, "For now I know that you fear God, and have not withheld your son, your favored, from Me." Then God said nothing. Abraham would have to figure out the purpose of the ram for himself. That was the test.

Abraham raised his eyes and saw the ram, created before the Creation of the world, whose one horn was the shofar used to create the world and whose other horn would announce the coming of the Messiah and the salvation of all the earth. Abraham saw the ram, and his eyes filled with tears—he wouldn't have to kill his beloved Isaac after all! The God who had given him the boy in the first place made it possible for the boy to live.

Awash in gratitude and in adoration, Abraham took the ram and offered it as an offering in place of his son.

Then Abraham named the site *Adonai Yireh*. He said to Isaac, "I was going to name this place *Yirat Adonai*, the fear of God, because that was the faith that summoned me to sacrifice you. But now I see that our God wants life. And I love that God! So I shall call the place *Adonai Yireh*, which means 'God sees.' Because God sees that our finest service is motivated by love."

And an angel from heaven, so pleased that the men now shared the angels' unending love for God, called out the promise: "God will bestow blessing upon you and make your descendants as numerous as the stars of heaven and the sands on the seashore. Because you know to serve God in love, to celebrate and sanctify your relationships of love, I will multiply your relationships until they shine a light that illuminates the world, until they cradle your step and guide humanity in its journey. And all the nations of the earth shall bless themselves by your descendants, because you understand what it is that God really wants, because you know who God really is."

But Sarah never lived to hear that blessing. When God realized the answer to Sarah's question, God sent an angel to bring her to the heavenly court. There God placed her on the throne of mercy and instructed her to plead on her children's behalf whenever God forgets Sarah's question: "Who are You?"

And on that day, Sarah and Abraham passed the test.

And so did God.

# Walking the Walk

## Tested by Our Deeds

I recall, as if it were yesterday, the times when Shira and Jacob—my then–two-year-old twins—were pushing the limits wherever they found them. When they were one, their big agenda item was walking. I'm sure you can recall young children learning to walk. Day after day they try to pull themselves up. Finally, they can stand holding onto some object of furniture or a well-placed knee. One day, after tremendous effort and lots of failures, the child eventually manages to balance and to walk independently.

Walking was a major accomplishment in my house during their first year, and in their second year, Jacob and Shira refused to walk anywhere—they ran! But I remember those first steps as though they had just happened. Proud parent that I was, I thrilled at my toddlers' achievement. Every parent, grandparent, aunt, and uncle can share a similar story of some adorable child who did some ordinary thing that felt extraordinary. And we can all recall our sense of pride and elation. I also recall feeling a little bit silly. After all, they had learned to walk yet I was bursting as though they each had been awarded the Nobel Prize!

What is most remarkable about those childhood achievements is that they are entirely predictable, completely normal, and we go bananas over them anyway. The vast preponderance of children eventually learn to walk, talk, climb stairs, draw, cut using scissors, and go to school as a matter of course. Intellectually, we know that our children will someday master all those challenges and more. Millions of children, all around the globe, accomplish those feats each year as they mature, so we might think that it's no big deal. Yet, when a child we love executes a new task, we respond as though it were a historical breakthrough of biblical proportions.

And, indeed, it is.

Every time someone lives up to his or her potential, every time one of us takes what used to be only possible and makes it actual, we do something miraculous. We make the world a different place. We make ourselves more than we had been earlier. What had only been a concept, an aspiration, or a goal has now become tangible, translated into the reality of deed. We—like God—are self-surpassing. There is a world of difference between our ambitions and our accomplishments, and there is ample precedent to favor what we actually do over what we merely aspire toward. As the ancient Rabbis teach, "Learning isn't the essential thing, the deed is" (*Ba-Midbar Rabbah, Naso* 14:10).

The story about Abraham's binding of Isaac is such a paradigm, urging us to translate our potential into deed, to transform what is merely possible into the actual. From this story, we can gain a deeper resolve to move beyond intention to action, beyond ephemeral desire to reliable achievement. In fact, so important is this biblical tale that the fifteenth-century sage Abravanel comments, "It constitutes the very reason for Israel's existence in the sight of our God in heaven" (*Commentary to the Torah*, Genesis 22:1).

## Defined by Our Deeds

God puts Abraham to a test, a *nisayon*. "Please take your son, your favored, whom you love, Isaac, and go to the land of Moriah, and offer him there as an offering" (Genesis 22:2).

God's request is shocking, bizarre, outrageous, and it calls for some explanation. Even though we have now read this story repeatedly, it never fails to ignite great fires of anger, puzzlement, and sorrow. What kind of a test is this? How can God instruct the aged, gentle patriarch to do such a thing? And who is the test for? Is it possible that God doesn't know what a *tzaddik*, a righteous person, Abraham is? The great fourteenth-century medieval commentator Rabbenu Nissim (in his *Perush Al Ha-Torah* to Genesis 22) insists, "The nature of this trial calls for explanation, since there is no doubt that the Holy One does not test a person in order to prove to God whether he is capable of withstanding the trial." And thirteenth-century philosopher Moses Maimonides affirms, "It should not be believed that the exalted God wants to test and try out a thing in order to know what God didn't know before" (*Guide for the Perplexed* 3:24).

God knows Abraham well enough to anticipate how Abraham will probably act. Therefore, it is unlikely that the purpose of the test is to teach God something new. But if the test isn't to show something to God, then to whom is the test addressed? Who needs to know how Abraham will respond to the divine request? What will be learned out of this anguished and outrageous process?

To answer that question, we need to look again at the event itself, to remind ourselves what we know about Abraham as a leader and as a man. Abraham, the great founder of the monotheistic faiths, the father of the Hebrews, is above all else a man of words and of lofty thoughts. His great contribution is his discovery of the one God who rules over Creation. As portrayed by the apocryphal *Book of Jubilees*, Abraham is a philosopher and a sage:

> Avram sat up during the night of the new moon of the seventh month, so that he might observe the stars from evening until daybreak so that he might see what the nature of the year would be with respect to rain. And he was sitting alone and making observations; and a word came into his heart, saying, "All of the signs of the stars and the signs of the sun and the moon are all in the hand of God. Why am I seeking? If God desires, God will make it rain morning and evening. And if God desires, God will not send rain. Everything is in God's hands." (12:16–18)

## Translating Ideas into Action

A man of contemplation and depth, Abraham lives in the realm of ideas. He studies the way the world works and derives from it the idea of a single God who is the very basis for all existence and for every living thing.

Just look at how fertile Abraham's ideas have been. That notion—that there is but one God in the world and that God is passionate about holiness and justice—has pretty much conquered humanity. Spirituality is resurgent throughout the globe, from the richest to the poorest lands, from the most educated to the least literate. The common heritage of a majority of humanity—religious and secular—stems from the contemplative insight of our father Abraham. While the words of the *Shema*, "Listen, Israel, the LORD is our God, the LORD is one" is the keystone affirmation of Judaism, its sentiment—that there is but one God—has become the credo of most of the world. Apparently, Abraham has good reason to put his confidence in ideas, to rely on the formulations of his mind rather than the workings of his hands.

God has to find a way to show Abraham that supreme value attaches not to concepts but to their implementation, that the worth of an idea is proved in the goodness and improvements that it can generate in the world and among society. It is what we do with our ideals that matters, not how often we express them or how deeply we feel them.

So God tests Abraham to show Abraham that the ideal of one loving God isn't worth very much unless we translate that love into practice, unless we have loved ones in whom we can cultivate God's image. In requesting that Abraham sacrifice Isaac for the sake of God, God hopes to move Abraham out of his ruminations and toward the realization of how precious his child—and every human being—is.

## From Words to Deeds

Even before the sacrifice is consummated, we see Abraham move from being a man of words to a man of deeds. When addressed by

God, Abraham answers with "Here I am" (Genesis 22:1). But once he is told what he must do, the normally loquacious man becomes solely a man of deeds. He almost never speaks throughout the three days that he and Isaac walk toward Mount Moriah, never speaks while building the altar or binding his son. In fact, Abraham is so absorbed in action, the doing of the deed, that the angel sent to stop the sacrifice has to call out not once, but twice, "Abraham! Abraham!" before Abraham will put down the knife and stop what he is doing.

In responding to God's call, we can picture Abraham—normally able to speak freely, usually given to deep thoughts—trapped in the anguish of having to make this most terrible of offerings to the God he serves. As he walks for three endless days, his mind must be racing through all sorts of possibilities—outright refusal, arguing with God, prayer, escape. But somewhere on that fateful journey, Abraham must see what is going on, must realize that this is indeed a test, a chance to show that he has learned something.

What Abraham learns is that action is the ultimate test of a person's beliefs. He learns that what we do in the world is the truest measure of our conviction, the best measure of our priorities. Up to this point in his life, Abraham can think of himself as a righteous man, but in his position, who wouldn't be? He has a wonderful wife, wealth, health, and an intimate relationship with the Holy Blessing One. And he has the promise of an even more glorious future through his beloved son Isaac. With so many gifts from God, Abraham can never be sure that his love for God isn't just a reasonable response to self-interest. How can he discover whether or not he really loves God without thought of reward? It takes the deed of the binding of Isaac to show him that his faith is real. It takes the action of binding his son to confirm the thoughts that have shaped his life.

In finding himself willing to sacrifice Isaac, Abraham learns the extent of his faith and his obedience to God. Abraham learns the profundity of his own conviction. As the thirteenth-century medieval Jewish scholar Rabbi Moses ben Nahman notes, "God confronts a person with the trial in order to translate into action the potentialities of one's character and to give reward of a good deed as well as for a good heart" (*Commentary to the Torah*, Genesis 22:1).

In fact, Abraham learns this lesson so well, this lesson of the power of deeds, that he never resumes his conversation with God. Traditional commentaries assume that the terminated dialogue is at God's insistence, and perhaps that is so. Perhaps God realizes that with this tenth trial, Abraham's last test, the patriarch has finally learned to rely less on grandiloquent speeches and more on tangible action. So maybe God stops talking because Abraham doesn't need the prompting any more. But I'd like to think that Abraham has learned the lesson of the test well enough that it is he who stops conversing. It is Abraham who then occupies himself with *mitzvot*, with living in the world— providing for Sarah's interment, remarrying, arranging for his son's betrothal. Armed with the knowledge that the only faith that matters is the faith that is manifest in our behavior, in how we treat each other, how we build a better and more sacred world, Abraham has no more need for long discussions. Abraham the public speaker has matured into Abraham the man of *ma'asim tovim*, good deeds. The binding of Isaac changes Abraham, and it offers to transform those of us willing to read it seriously and to take its lessons to heart.

## The Lessons of the Test

What do we learn from Abraham's test?

We learn to judge and to measure our own beliefs by the behavior they motivate, not by the words we wrap them in. Giving to the poor is how we show that we believe in *tzedakah*. Volunteering our time and our resources to the congregation or to other charities is how we know we care about healing the world. Treating the members of our family with decency and love is the evidence that we savor domestic tranquility. And engaging in spiritual learning and the performance of acts of holiness and righteousness is the sign that we are proud of being people of faith. As the fifteenth-century medieval philosopher and rabbi Joseph Albo reminds us, "One who has not performed deeds of valor … cannot be compared to one who has … actually performed these deeds…. Every action leaves its own indelible mark on the performer. This practice in good deeds is called *nisayon*, a test" (*Sefer Ha-Ikkarim 4*, 13:127). The sum total of what we do creates the portrait of what we truly value.

Abravanel's claim that this biblical story constitutes our reason for being makes sense when we derive from it the lesson that action speaks louder than words. However important ideas may be for motivating righteous behavior, the fruit of pious living lies in the kinds of communities we maintain, the way we treat the weakest and the neediest in our midst, how we make each participant feel welcome. As the eighteenth-century rabbi Solomon Dubno notes in his introduction to the *Bi'ur*:

> A person's character in the sphere of practical action cannot be perfected by a theoretical knowledge of goodness. This must be realized by habitual action so that good deeds become second nature.

That second nature, in fact, is what is cultivated through the constant repetition of the sacred tasks that Judaism understands as *mitzvot*. How very significant that we, like Abraham, translate the sense of being tested, of being commanded by God, into palpable practices for all to see. As important as theology and philosophy may be to discerning the proper path, we can only walk the way of faith through concrete acts, through deeds of loving-kindness and holiness. As the twentieth-century theologian Abraham Joshua Heschel reminds us:

> Religion is not a feeling for the mystery of living, or a sense of awe, wonder, or fear, which is the root of religion; but rather the question what to do with the feeling for the mystery of living, what to do with the awe, wonder, or fear. (*God in Search of Man*, 112)

# Integrity

## Hearing the Voice of God

I n the story of the *Akedah*, while it is clear that Abraham is tested and Isaac is to be the sacrifice, we might learn something useful by revisiting God's role in the drama. Let's focus on one particular question: Precisely who does the testing? Who summons Abraham to murder his son?

The Bible tells us, "*Ha-Elohim nisah et Avraham*—Elohim tested Abraham" (Genesis 22:1). Conventionally translated as "God," the Hebrew word *ha-Elohim* technically means "the gods" (one *el;* many *elohim*). This insight, offered by twentieth-century spiritual leader Rabbi Michael Lerner in his book *Jewish Renewal*, opens up a way to understand why Abraham—usually so willing to argue for a just cause—so readily acquiesces to this obscene test. Such a focus might sensitize us to how the God of Israel acts to shatter complacency and to offer hope. When Abraham hears *ha-elohim*, the gods, he hears the conventional powers of his age. And he hears the force of convention commanding him to sacrifice his son to prove his integrity, to prove that he belongs.

Abraham hears a compelling voice, and he is far from the last mortal to acquiesce to such a demand. We all feel compelled to do things that make us uneasy. Our lives and our civilization require us to willingly submit to the voices of various norms, the internalized authorities that tell us, "Just go along and do it; everybody else does." Haven't we all felt that pressure in our lives, the entire weight of family and culture and habit pushing us toward actions we would otherwise not take, making us act in ways that we would, ideally, resist? We perpetuate this "objective" coercion in ways both little and big: when arguing with children about what they have to wear, we insist they must don an unwanted garment because that's how people dress when they go to ... Haven't we all heard ourselves stop children from doing something they want to with the line "Little girls don't do that" or "Little boys don't play with that; it's for girls." And so the internalized voice uses our own voice to sound objective, as though the demanded action were built into the nature of the cosmos, beyond dispute or hope. It starts pushing us from our earliest childhood, telling us, "But you have to do it this way. This is how it's always been done. This is how everybody does it."

As we grow, that same voice continues to command us, telling us what is worthy of recognition and what is not. The voice tells us that excelling in literature is for nerds but excelling in athletics is the key to popularity. The voice tells us that knitting and sewing are mere craft while painting and sculpting constitute high art. It tells us that there is one right way to develop, that there are skills that make parents smile and other skills that don't. Some strengths make you a teacher's favorite, and other strengths don't. And so we are pushed and shaped and forced throughout our childhood, throughout our schooling, to become something different than what we are inside. Instead of being nurtured so we can blossom, we are sculpted to accord to someone else's vision.

The forces that make us deny our own inner gifts don't stop with childhood. The pursuit of our own well-being, financial security, and professional prestige makes us do all kinds of things that we otherwise would not do. A small inner voice may even occasionally acknowledge that our acquiescence is ridiculous and yet we do it because, well, everybody does it. That's the way the world works and it's always been done that way. We go along because the voice seems too strong to resist.

Abraham lived in a time when some societies showed their devotion to the gods by murdering their children. Archaeologists have excavated the mass sacrificial graves of scores of infants in Carthage,

Phoenicia, and other places. Don't think they did it joyously or easily; this sacrifice was meant to hurt. How else would the gods know how much the rich and powerful loved them if these people didn't give their deities what they most cherished?

That was the way the world had always worked; that was the way people did things. So Abraham isn't surprised when *ha-Elohim* says to him, "Please take your son, your favored, whom you love, Isaac, and go to the land of Moriah, and offer him there as an offering on one of the mountains that I will tell you." Abraham must have rationalized, "I'm a spiritual leader, I need to do what everyone expects of me. This call from God is no different from the call that other leaders get. My mission is so important that it's worth some personal sacrifice. I need to do the responsible thing." And so Abraham does, although he has the decency, at least, not to speak. For three days he walks in silence because, in the face of that commanding voice, there is nothing reasonable to say in response. Three days later his beloved son is strapped to the altar, and Abraham picks up the knife in conformity to what he and his society perceive to be the commanding voice of God.

## A New Vision of Spirit

That's the moment when a radically new vision of spirit erupts into the world. Because at that point it is no longer *ha-Elohim* who speaks to Abraham. It is suddenly, redemptively, Y-H-V-H, pronounced "Adonai" and often translated as "LORD." "The voice of Adonai is power; the voice of the LORD is majesty" (Psalm 29:4). That voice also shatters complacency, habit, and social convention. It is the thundering voice of the God who will be revealed to Moses and to the Jewish people at Sinai. It is the God who insists that all people are made in the divine image. It is the God who mandates loving our neighbor as ourselves and commands us to care for the weak, the hungry, the widowed, and the orphaned. It is the Compassionate One who is revealed in glory. The God of Israel offers new possibility, new hope: things can be done differently. And they must.

The angel of Adonai says, "Abraham! Abraham!" And Abraham says, "Here I am." Then the God of Israel commands, "Do not send your hand against the lad, and do nothing to him." That is the shattering voice of the God of Israel. We serve a God who abhors human suffering.

Our God doesn't care whether it was always done a certain way. Our God isn't impressed simply because everybody else does it. Our God doesn't recognize that injustice, mendacity, or selfishness is necessary to get ahead. Our God insists that we can do better, that we must become better. The God of Israel fosters dissatisfaction with the complacency of the world as it is: "Those who love Adonai hate evil," (Psalm 97:10). Our God offers a vision of what the world ought to be: a world in which parents don't hurt their children, people can trust each other at the deepest level, and the pursuit of peace and justice is our highest ideal and the crowning service of God. That is the world that we are commanded to establish: "And none shall hurt or destroy on all My holy mountain" (Isaiah 11:9).

The story of the test of Abraham is the story of rejecting the voice of accommodation, though many mistake it for the voice of God. Too often in our world, we hear that voice in the idolatry of youth, looks, money, sex, self-interest, and power. These are the same false gods before whom humanity has always groveled and for whom we have always been so willing to sacrifice our children and our decency.

Then as now, the God of Israel, the God who spoke to Abraham and Sarah, the God who was revealed to Isaac and Rebecca, the God who was shown at the top of Mount Sinai and who gave us the Ten Commandments, Adonai, despises those idolatries. Then as now, our God calls out, and says, "My children! Stop! Don't harm the child." When we attend to that sacred call, we, too, can pass Abraham's test of integrity.

〰〰〰

# Resilience

## We Can Learn from Our Trials

How life teaches us! We read the wisdom of books and study the lectures of professors and we think we are ready for what life sends our way. Armed with our learning, we venture into the world and discover that the constructs of the mind don't help bind the wounds of the heart.

I remember the first time I went into a hospital room to counsel someone who was dying of a terminal illness. I was accompanied by a wise chaplain with many years of experience. We stood by the patient's bedside and I expected that we would commiserate with his plight. We would explain that this illness wasn't a punishment from God, but that these tragedies are random. With the inexperience of youth, I believed that nothing good can ever come from pain, that suffering is but an enemy to be vanquished, never a teacher to be heeded.

Imagine my horror, then, when the chaplain turned to the patient and asked, "What has your cancer taught you?" And imagine my surprise when the patient responded by offering many valuable lessons that he derived from his illness: renewed love of life, better priorities, deeper love for his family. This man knew exactly what the chaplain was asking, and he was able to share the precious insights that he had gained at a very high price.

Another memory: when I was fourteen I was diagnosed with a terminal, inoperable cancer. Having endured two years of terrible pain, a pain so embarrassing that I hid it from my family throughout that period, I finally couldn't take it anymore. Once I revealed my suffering to my parents, they rushed me to a doctor, who promptly hospitalized me. There I was poked and prodded by countless experts, each trying to get a fix on my malady and to decide on a course of action to address it. Thank God, one clever dermatologist noticed some bumps on my arm and connected that to my internal affliction. Within two weeks I was undergoing rounds of chemo and radiation therapy that lasted for several months.

I'm pleased to tell you that the assessment that my cancer was terminal and inoperable turned out to be an exaggeration. But the pain and fear I felt were not. I would gladly never have confronted that trial, never have suffered that anguish. But I also know that I could not be the rabbi, counselor, husband, father, or friend I am today were it not for the lessons I learned from my own brush with death and pain.

The truth is that we all suffer at different points in our lives. Each of us faces challenges and endures pain—both our own and that of our loved ones. As creatures who are finite, mortal, and flawed, it is not ours to choose whether or not we suffer. But we do have the power to choose how to respond. We may not be the masters of our fate, but we are the captains of our own souls.

It is now in this light that I would like us to think about the binding of Isaac.

Whenever we encounter this story, it makes us profoundly uncomfortable. Part of our struggle, no doubt, is that we object to a God who demands the sacrifice of what we love most. We hate that Abraham is called to demonstrate faithfulness by offering up his beloved son. We resent the imposition of suffering in a world that is too filled with pain and sorrow. Abraham, as our tradition recognizes, is a stand-in for each one of us. As the Talmud notes, "Sound a ram's horn before Me so that I remember on your behalf the binding of Isaac and count it to you as though you had bound yourselves before Me" (Rosh Ha-Shanah 16a). The trial of Abraham tries us all. In his silent anguish we feel an echo of our own pain.

# Our Response to Suffering

Just like Abraham, we, too, must concede that life puts us on trial. Much as we might wish to determine our own destiny, such control is not in our hands. We cannot choose whether we will suffer or not, but we can decide what to do with our suffering.

Abraham, our father, also faced such a choice. The Bible records, "God tested Abraham" (Genesis 22:1). Abraham has no exemption from suffering; indeed, his righteousness makes him even more aware of his own pain. As the Midrash notes, "God tests the faith of the righteous in that God reveals to them only at a later time the ultimate meaning of the trials to which they are subjected" (*Bereshit Rabbah* 55:7). Like the rest of us, all Abraham feels is anguish and sorrow. In the midst of his suffering, he cannot discern purpose or pattern. Only pain.

In his experience of pain, he is no different from any other human being. Indeed, the Zohar recognizes that to live is to lose, that to be is to suffer and to grieve: "Rabbi Shimon said: We have learned that the expression 'And it came to pass in the days of' denotes sorrow, while the expression 'And it came to pass' even without 'in the days of' is still tinged with sorrow" (I:119b).

*Tinged with sorrow.* I can't think of a better description of what it feels like to be alive. We know that the dominant flavor of life is bitter-sweet— even in our moments of greatest joy, we recall our losses. Even in our greatest grief, we draw consolation from our love and our hope.

Yet this test need not shatter us; being tried doesn't have to destroy us. Interestingly, the biblical word for test, *nisayon*, means "experience" or "experiment" in Modern Hebrew. We alone can transform our test into an experience—something that provides an opportunity for new understandings and deeper connections. With the right attitude, our trials can transform us. The nineteenth-century philosopher Friedrich Nietzsche said, "What does not kill me makes me stronger." Our father Abraham learned a similar lesson. I think he would have said, "What doesn't kill me can make me wiser and more compassionate."

Why is Abraham's resilience tested? We are never told. One possibility, however, is that suffering was a necessary—if regrettable—spur to depth, caring, and meaning. Throughout his life, Abraham has known only success: a beautiful and devoted wife, great wealth, prominence, and intimacy with the Creator of the Universe. With all that bounty, how can he learn to empathize with others? How can he not feel smug and superior to other people with their failures and their sorrows? How can he not blame them for their sorrow? Suffering teaches Abraham what success cannot. The Zohar notes this salutary function when it asks, "Why is it written that God tested Abraham and not Isaac? It had to be Abraham! He had to be crowned with rigor…. Abraham was not complete until now" (119b).

Perhaps the worth of Abraham's trial lay in adding a layer of depth to his faith. How easy it is—when all goes well—to put God in our pocket, to think of God as a big buddy, a Santa in the sky. How tempting it is to think of God as merely there to indulge our obsession with ourselves! Suffering makes such a narcissistic and arrogant faith impossible. By undergoing the ordeal of his trial, Abraham transcends the bartering faith of his youth and reaches the more nuanced trustfulness of mature faith. As the psalmist sings: "You who have made me undergo many troubles and misfortunes will revive me again…. You will turn and comfort me" (Psalm 71:20–21). While faith doesn't exempt us from tragedy, it does provide comfort even amid the pain. Abraham learns that faithfulness between God and humanity is not wish fulfillment. It is commitment, relationship, and steadfastness.

The Bible records no reason for Abraham's trial. And few of us ever know why we must endure suffering and sorrow. But we do know that how we respond to our suffering has the power to transform us, for good or for ill. As twentieth-century spiritual leader Rabbi Mordecai Kaplan notes, "According to Jewish traditional teaching, a person is not trapped but tested. Our vicissitudes should serve as a challenge to our faith…. To deny the worth of life and to fall into despair because the promise is slow of fulfillment is to fail the test"

(*Meaning of God in Modern Jewish Religion*, 68). How we cope with the trials of life spells the difference between renewal and resignation, between spiritual growth and spiritual stagnation.

Abraham's greatness lies precisely in his determination to respond to his trial with resilience and resolve. God calls out the test, and Abraham does not evade the challenge. His immediate answer is "*Hineni—Here I am.*" Abraham's willingness to set out on this gruesome path is rooted in faithfulness—to Isaac, to himself, and to his God. In the words of twentieth-century Bible scholar Rabbi Julian Morgenstern, "This is the true faith, which enables us to endure all trials and stand all tests, and prove ourselves fit and ready for the great work for which, sooner or later, God calls everyone of us," (*The Book of Genesis*).

Abraham passes the test because he faces the challenge that is posed to him. Rather than fleeing what lies ahead, rather than cowering and allowing its struggle to cripple him, Abraham moves forward to do whatever needs to be done, to go wherever it is that his path in life will lead.

## Life Lessons

Abraham learns that suffering—as painful as it is—can be a source of insight. It is in this spirit that the thirteenth-century medieval Jewish scholar Rabbi Moses ben Nahman asserts, "All trials in the Torah are for the good of the one who is being tried" (*Commentary on the Torah*, Genesis 22:1). Not that pain is good—true faith doesn't celebrate misery. We don't seek out suffering, and we certainly don't enjoy it. But neither do we refuse to learn from life's challenges. In the words of the Jerusalem Talmud, "Why do you scorn suffering?" (Peah 8:9). The great men and women of the Torah were able use their trials to derive great lessons about life. They wrestled with their pain and emerged wiser and better because of how they responded to those trials. In that sense—and in that sense alone—their trials were for their benefit. They used those trials as sources of deeper understanding and connection.

Abraham learned from his trial, and it became a springboard for personal growth and spiritual depth. The Zohar recognizes a hint of that growth from the way the angel calls out his name as Abraham is about to slaughter his son. At the moment when Isaac is bound to the altar, as Abraham raises the knife high in the air, "An angel of the LORD called to him from the heavens and said, 'Abraham! Abraham!'"

Why does the angel repeat Abraham's name twice? "Rebbe Hiyya said that the angel repeated Abraham's name in order to animate him with a new spirit and to spur him to new activity with a new heart" (Zohar 119b). Having faced his suffering directly, having been willing to learn from his terrible trial, Abraham emerges with a new spirit and a new heart. Indeed, the Zohar claims that the angels shouted, "Abraham! Abraham!" to show that "the latter Abraham was not like the former Abraham; the latter was the perfected Abraham, while the former was still incomplete" (Zohar 119b). Out of the horror of his suffering, Abraham changes. Abraham grows.

"God tries everyone in some way…. The real test is the way we offer our sacrifice, the willingness with which we give up what is dear, the perfect faith in God which we still preserve, and which keeps us from doubting God's wisdom and goodness" (*The Book of Genesis*, 148). These words of Rabbi Morgenstern, written almost a century ago, translate the great lesson of the test of Abraham: we do not seek to suffer. We do not deify pain. But we know that suffering and pain are part of the journey we call life, and we know that we can learn—and grow—even from an encounter with tragedy, especially from the trials life brings.

# Responsibility

## What We Sacrifice for Our Parents

We like to think that our lives are our own.

After all, we citizens of the United States live in a country that assures us that we are "endowed by our Creator with certain inalienable rights, that among these rights are life, liberty, and the pursuit of happiness." Our right to pursue happiness is a personal declaration of independence—no one else knows what can make each of us happy, so no one else should run our lives for us. No one else force us to do something against our will.

This radical autonomy, living our lives as we choose, is the great idolatry of our age and a source of great loneliness and unhappiness. Far from being distinct creatures—each of us separately finding happiness by pursuing our own personal agenda—human beings were made to be social, to blossom in the company of others. I am not simply myself, but I become myself by being someone's son, brother, husband, father, uncle, friend, rabbi, and more. We are who we are because of who we are with others. Perhaps that is why the Bible teaches us, "It is with the multitude of people that the Sovereign's glory is to be found" (Proverbs 14:28).

If our personal identity unfolds only in relation to other people, then no one has pride of place more than our parents. The people who brought us into the world, who cared for us when we were incapable of caring for ourselves, who fed and sheltered us as infants, and who taught us how to behave and think and care as children—these people surely have the greatest claim to our hearts and our lives. Yet, instead, how often do we think of our mothers and fathers in terms of what they owe us and what we need from them? It is an odd form of flattery that children—even adult children—feel entitled to their parents' endless love and support.

There is a great deal of truth to that expectation. Precisely because they have been so involved in their children's infancy and childhood, parents are connected to their children in an overpowering way. The ancient Sages understood the biblical phrase "as your own soul" as a reference "to one's father" (*Sifre Devarim, Piska* 87), so deeply enmeshed in our hearts are our parents.

That involvement is not reciprocal. Even as children turn to their parents to fulfill their expectations, we are surprised (and often resentful) of the expectations that parents themselves present. Parents may be intrusive. Parents may be nosy. Parents may have different ideas about how their children should conduct their lives. Small surprise, then, that some of our deepest ties are to our parents, but so are our deepest conflicts.

## Deeds of the Parents

The binding of Isaac is a story about how a father intrudes into the life of his son, and of how his son accepts the sacrifice that only he can give his father. "The deeds of the parents are signs for the children" (Talmud, Sotah 34a). We can learn how to treat our own parents by examining how Isaac deals with his own needy dad.

This tight little story is among the most powerful in the Bible, in part because of what it says about the relationship between parents and children and the expectations that parents and children impose on each other. Twentieth-century literary critic Erich Auerbach calls the binding of Isaac "a story fraught with background" (*Mimesis*, 12). Scurrying around the background of this terrifying tale are our own feelings about what we owe our parents and our children, our disappointments and delights, how we have been nurtured and neglected, how we nurture and fail to nurture as well. Auerbach observes, "Since so much in the story is dark and incomplete, and since the reader knows that God is a hidden God, his efforts to interpret it constantly find something new to feed upon" (*Mimesis*, 15).

The story begins with an eruption. Out of nowhere, God addresses Abraham with a shattering demand: "Take your beloved son, Isaac, and bring him as a burnt offering at the place that I will show you." Ever the obedient servant, Abraham hastens to fulfill God's decree, saddling his donkey, mustering two servants, and heading out with his dear son, Isaac. For three days they walk in complete silence. No words intrude upon the dread and terror of where they are heading, of what Abraham must do. As if to make sure that we don't miss the focus on the relationship between parent and child, the Torah repeats the word *ben*, "son," nine times in the first fourteen short verses. The word *ahavah*, "love," is mentioned for the very first time in the Bible in this story, and it is used to describe what a parent feels for a child, what Abraham feels for Isaac.

And then, at the very center of the story, we find the only recorded discussion between Abraham and Isaac. The only time they ever converse with each other is to discuss the place of sacrifice in their relationship:

"My father!" says Isaac.

"Here I am, my son," responds Abraham.

"Here is the flame and the wood; but where is the sheep for the burnt offering?"

As we know, Isaac was thirty-seven-years-old (*Midrash Va-Yosha* 36), old enough to overpower an old father, and old enough to notice that something isn't kosher about this offering. So Isaac asks. And his father's answer is enigmatic at best: "God will provide the sheep for the offering, my son."

Abraham's words are true in ways that even he does not appreciate. God will indeed provide a sheep for the slaughter. But what Abraham means by this is that God's choice of an offering is already determined, and the "sheep" in question is Isaac. Indeed, the Zohar notices that

Abraham should have said, "God will provide for us" rather than "God will provide the sheep" (120a). Why did Abraham phrase it so awkwardly? What he meant was God will provide for Himself when necessary. But for the present it is going to be my son and nothing else.

For the binding of Isaac to count as a test, for Abraham to truly be tested, he must believe that God wants him to slaughter Isaac. He must willingly sacrifice what is most precious to him, his son. Without that belief, there would be no test for Abraham, just a charade.

## Deeds of the Children

But what of Isaac? What is his role in his father's drama? I'd like to suggest that Isaac knew what was going on. He breaks the silence to point out that there is no sheep for the slaughter, hinting that the grim truth is already dawning on him. Abraham's answer must have confirmed his hunch. Again, the Zohar shares this understanding:

> Here we must reflect that the Torah says, "God tested Abraham." The verse should have read, "God tested Isaac," for Isaac was already thirty-seven years old and his father was no longer accountable for him. If Isaac had said "I refuse," his father would not have been punished.... (119b)

The Zohar realizes that Isaac had the power to nullify Abraham's test. All he had to do was to refuse to participate and this last, greatest encounter between God and Abraham would have been impossible. Indeed, the Kabbalah, the mystical strain of Judaism, credits Isaac as the hidden hero of the binding. According to the Zohar, "All the angels wept when they saw Abraham binding Isaac, the upper and lower beings trembled and shook, and all on account of Isaac" (120a). Note: on account of *Isaac*. His grandeur is the cause of their marvel. Or, consider again:

> Rabbi Judah said, "Isaac purified himself and in intention offered himself up to God. At that moment, he was etherealized and, as it

were, he ascended to the throne of God like the odor of the incense
of spices that the priests offered to God twice a day." (Zohar 120a)

For the Kabbalistic tradition, what makes Isaac the hero is his willingness to allow himself to become a sacrifice for the sake of his
father. That understanding appears in the Midrash as well, where we
find a debate between Isaac and his brother Ishmael about whose love
for God is greater. Ishmael claims that his love for God is superior,
because he had allowed himself to be circumcised at the age of thir-
teen, an act of great devotion for a boy of that age! Not to be outdone,
Isaac exclaims:

> "All that you did lend to the Holy Blessing One was three drops
> of blood. But I am now thirty-seven years old, yet if God desired
> of me that I be slaughtered, I would not refuse." Said the Holy
> Blessing One, "This is the moment!" Straightaway, "God tested
> Abraham." (*Bereshit Rabbah* 54:4)

The Talmud also hints at Isaac's awareness when it asks:

> Why does one blow a shofar taken from a ram? The Holy Bless-
> ing One said, "Blow a ram's horn before Me so that I recall in
> your favor the binding of Isaac, son of Abraham, and count it to
> you as though you had bound yourselves before Me." (Rosh Ha-
> Shanah 16a)

Note that what we—the children of Abraham—get credit for acting
like Isaac, for binding ourselves, not for what Abraham does. Note
also that the Talmud refers to this incident as "the binding of Isaac,"
not the trial of Abraham. Only if Isaac knew what he was doing, only
if he submitted voluntarily, would this recognition make any sense.
Indeed, it is Isaac's willingness to be sacrificed that the Torah itself
recognizes when, immediately after their brief conversation, we are
told of Abraham and Isaac, "And the two walked together."

They walked together as one, united in a common purpose.

# From Generation to Generation

So Isaac knew. He knew that God was testing his father; he knew that he was to be his father's sacrifice; he knew that the glory and the attention would go to his father. Yet he walked on with his father toward their goal. He made his father's goal his own. Why?

The reason Isaac's willingness to go with his father matters is because we, too, are called upon to make sacrifices for our parents. All of us are summoned to play the part of supporting actor or actress in the drama of our parents' lives. We are all called to be willing to sacrifice so that they might pass the tests that they encounter in life.

Our parents' tests come at every stage of our lives: the little child who must occasionally sacrifice her parents' attention for the sake of a younger sibling; the teenager who must sacrifice some independence and control for the sake of a parent's concern and standards; the young adult who must spend time away from friends or preferred activities in order to attend to his parents' needs to stay in touch; and the middle-aged (and sometimes elderly) adult who must sacrifice time, worry, and finances for parents who might be ill, lonely, or declining.

At each step of our lives, we find ourselves connected to people we did not choose, indebted to people whose decisions we can't control, people we love intensely and dearly, whose approval we crave, whose love we need, whose grasp we both desire and evade. All of us are someone's children. Those of us who are also parents know this drama from the other side, too: our parental need to be involved in our children's lives, our need for communication and for touch, our need for our own lives and for a measure of independence from our adult children. We know that none of us gets to control our own lives; none of us determines, in the words of the High Holy Day prayer book, "who shall live and who shall die."

At each step of the way, parents and children engage in a dynamic minuet, a give-and-take of giving and needing, insisting and relinquishing. For children, finding the balance between living their lives in accordance with their own integrity while also giving up some independence to please their parents reflects a real struggle and a sacrifice. Allowing older parents to have their own integrity and to live their own lives requires a sacrifice no less difficult. Above all else, being willing to act as support and ally in the parents' ongoing journey through life takes devotion, discipline, and a willingness on the part of the children to sublimate their own needs for the well-being of their parents.

But don't our parents deserve that? Having given of themselves throughout our childhood and our adolescence, don't they deserve some measure of sacrifice from their children? Doesn't that willingness to surrender for our parents offer us something in return? "Though my father and my mother forsake me, the LORD will gather me in" (Psalm 27:10).

The Zohar sees the growth that comes through self-sacrifice as the great hidden message of the binding of Isaac:

> Come and see the secret of one word: Even though we have said that Abraham, not Isaac, is designated by the biblical verse, Isaac is secretly implied, for it is written, *Elohim nisah et Avraham*—God tested Abraham. It is precisely this *et* that refers to Isaac. For until now, Isaac was dwelling in the sphere of low power. But as soon as he was bound on the altar, initiated into *Din/Gevurah* by Abraham, he was arrayed in his own sphere alongside Abraham. (102a)

In other words, when Isaac perceives only his own needs as primary, he is still a child—emotionally, if not physically. When he is able to sublimate his own desire for the sake of his father, when he can become a parent for his parent, then he ascends from a lower spiritual level to a higher one. Isaac acquires the attribute of *gevurah*, heroism, through his willingness to sacrifice for his father's needs.

In every generation, in each family, that ancient drama continually unfolds. Can children grow to take their parents' needs into account? Can they learn to show the same tender consideration for their parents that a parent shows for a child?

You never stop being a child in relation to your parents. But you can become, in addition to a child, something more—a friend, a support, an advocate. By taking on the role of parent for our own parents, our souls blossom and expand in areas we never dreamed possible. We demonstrate a capacity to grow in the expression of love, in our steadfastness and in our faithfulness.

In that regard, by sacrificing for the people from whom we expect sacrifice, in caring for the people from whom—as children—we felt entitled to boundless love and support, we can transcend a sense of neediness and an emotional impoverishment that such an attitude can foster. By learning to give, we learn that we can give and that we have what's needed to give.

In discovering that inner bounty—of spirit, love, and care—we reveal our own godliness more fully. Made in God's image, we, like God, are capable of unending love. The more we give that love away, the more richly we are nourished, the more aware we become of our own inner strength and abundance.

The more we love, the more we receive love. And who deserves love more than our parents?

# Joy

## Is It Okay to Love Life?

In every age, life comes at us whole: filled with moments of joy and of sorrow, offering exultation and grief. We do not get to choose what faces us at each moment, but we do have the capacity to be self-determining, to decide which future we work toward, to face life with a spirit of resolute optimism or to surrender to despair. That stark reality faced Abraham in his trial. Would he use that occasion to craft deeper meaning in his life? Would he choose to affirm the insoluble bond linking him with his beloved son? Would he respond in such a way that his deepest affirmations walked with him through that silent hell and returned again with him into the eerie new dawn? Isaac also faced a stark choice: would he spend the rest of his days as a shadow of his former self, a lifelong victim of his moment under the knife? Or would he respond to God's invitation to renewed life and somehow find the strength to recapture love, belonging, and joy?

As with so many of our human choices, how we understand the world around us and how we hold on to community, values, and vision can determine whether we will survive the situations that life throws our way.

This, too, is an era during which we are called on to focus on the large issues of life and death, of human frailty and resilience, on what our purpose on this planet is, and on how we are using (and on how we are meant to use) our time. Life offers a natural invitation to look inward, to stand before God in our nakedness, which is to say in complete honesty, unfeigned, as we truly are. We are bidden to take stock of our strengths and to honestly assess the challenges that still remain. This is true for us, both as individuals and as members of the Jewish people, just as it was for our fathers, Abraham and Isaac.

There are certain moments that focus our attention in ways we might not anticipate. The summer of 2006 was such a time for me. As Israel's north was bombarded by missiles from Iranian- and Syrian-supplied Hezbollah attacks, as well as from the still–newly independent Palestinian Authority, which included the terrorist group Hamas in its government, democratic Israel responded to the final straw of the abduction of its soldiers with a massive military response against Lebanon that left hundreds of thousands of refugees and resulted in a large number of civilian deaths. The complexity and tragedies of the violence consumed most rabbinic sermons that Rosh Ha-Shanah and Yom Kippur. But not mine. What I focused on was a quotation that came out of the crisis, one that reveals a deeper and more abiding clash of values that still requires our focused attention.

In the days leading up to the outbreak, the *Los Angeles Times* published this quotation from an unnamed Hezbollah guard: "People are begging Sheik Hassan Nasrallah to fight," he said. "They want to be human bombs. This is the difference between us and them. They fear death and love life. We are believers in another life, and we welcome death" (July 15, 2006).

Jews "fear death and love life," claims a self-appointed enemy of the Jews. He believes that assertion to be insulting, as if there were something wrong with Jews because we love life. I think his description is correct: we do, indeed, love life. So the question remains: is that such a terrible thing? Is it a moral or religious lapse to love life? Is that love a betrayal of God or religion or humanity?

## The Religious Obligation to Love Life

On the factual level, this nameless guard is correct—the Jewish religion explicitly mandates the love of life:

Who is it who desires life and loves long days, in order to see good?
Keep your tongue from evil, and your lips from speaking guile.
Depart from evil, and do good; seek peace, and pursue it.
(Psalm 34:13–15)

The psalmist recognizes that desiring life and loving long years entail moral commitments to ourself, other human beings, and Creation. It is precisely because we desire life that we refrain from speaking ill of others, that we seek peace and pursue it, that we depart from evil and do good. The love of life ought, and in Jewish terms is understood, to inspire righteousness, goodness, and engagement with our fellow human beings. The Talmud tells us, "Grab and eat, grab and drink, because this world from which we depart is like a wedding feast" (Eruvin 54a). A wedding feast—what a sumptuous image for life itself! We have all been summoned to a magnificent party, a glorious feast that we didn't have to prepare, but one that was already set up for our enjoyment. Our only task is to revel in its joy, to marvel in its beauty, to acknowledge its wonder and its delight.

The insistence on loving life reflects a solid theological commitment. *Sefer Bereshit*, the book of Genesis, opens the Torah with the repeated reminder that God assesses each day's creation as *ki tov*, "it is good," and finally celebrates the totality of Creation as *ki tov me'od*, "it is very good." To refrain from enjoying life is to spurn God's sweet gift, it is to rebel against God's judgment on such a fundamental issue as the magnificence of being itself. Small wonder, then, that ninth-century Jewish philosopher Sa'adia Gaon reminds us, in his magisterial *Sefer Emunot ve-De'ot*, "The first of God's acts of kindness toward all creatures was the gift of existence." It may well be that some other traditions understand life to be a curse and an imposition, our poor benighted souls exiled from a place of purity to become enmeshed in the dross of carnal existence. But not us; we understand God's birthing us into the material world as a boon and a blessing. The philosopher and theologian Franz Rosenzweig articulates deep Jewish insight when he writes, "Life is not the most precious of all things; nevertheless it is beautiful" (*Understanding the Sick and the Healthy*, 63).

## A Behavioral Imperative

Delighting in life is more than a theoretical truth—it constitutes a behavioral imperative woven throughout the strands of Jewish deed. It forms the anchor that gives the binding of Isaac its poignancy and the trial of Abraham its sting. The Halakhah repeatedly directs our attention to the religious beauty of life and the behavioral expression of its appreciation. "Nothing stands in the way of saving a life outside of idolatry, illicit relations, or murder" (Talmud, Yoma 82a, Sanhedrin 74a). The Halakhah famously limits which sins a person can seek to avoid through recourse to suicide to these three. Why? Because our ancestors were all too aware of worldviews that think it is a mark of depth or piety to take one's own life. After all, what better way could there be to show love of God than to shed this material coil? And the religion forbids it. The clarity of that break with an otherworldly orientation erupts at the very pinnacle of the *Akedah*, as Abraham raises his knife to sacrifice his beloved son.

> An angel of the LORD called to him from the heavens and said, "Abraham! Abraham!" He said, "Here I am." He said, "Do not send your hand against the lad, and do nothing to him. For now I know that you fear God, and have not withheld your son, your favored, from Me." (Genesis 22:11–12)

Sacrificing our loved ones is not the way. Despising their lives, or our own, is not permitted. Separating spirit from body is antithetical to the world-embracing, life-loving spirituality that resonates throughout Jewish life. Direct intervention, and with great haste, conveys the good news that God wants Isaac to live, wants us all to live:

> The Holy Blessing One said to the archangel Michael, "Why do you stand still? Do not let Abraham continue!" Michael began calling Abraham ... in rapid succession ... and like a person crying out in

sharp distress, the angel burst out at him: "What are you doing? *Do not send your hand against the lad!* (*Pesikta Rabbati* 40)

We are commanded to honor life above virtually every commandment. The Talmud elsewhere instructs us, "In cases where the issue is the preservation of life you are obligated to rule leniently" (Yoma 83a), meaning the ruling that best ensures the successful preservation of life. The Sages of the Talmud, in commenting on the verse in Leviticus, "You shall live by them" (18:5), adds the mandate "You should not die by them" (Yoma 85a). The *mitzvot*, according to this reading, are not intended to restrict our life, but to enhance our living. The observance of *mitzvot* allows us to appreciate beauty more profoundly, makes us attentive to the passage of time and its sacred seasons, connects us to our fellow human beings, and requires us to come to the aid of one another. The *mitzvot* are not there to remove us from the mainstream of life, but rather allow us to immerse ourselves in its flow. This link between life and religious affirmation is why the Talmud reveals, "Once a person dies, that person is free of *mitzvot*" (Shabbat 30a). *Mitzvot* and life: these entwined gifts are to be cherished. They are to be celebrated. Like Abraham, we are commanded to embrace life.

## From Anger and Fear to Acceptance, Laughter, and Joy

The unnamed Hezbollah guard had it all wrong. If I had a chance to speak to him, I would have read him wise words from my son Jacob. Jacob has struggled with the impact of autism his entire life. At the age of fourteen, he reached a watershed in his understanding and a response to his disability. Here's what I'd share with the Hezbollah guard who was so perversely proud to welcome death:

> For most of my life, my existence was controlled by autism. Autism was at the root of every experience I had or didn't have. I lived with constant anger at my disability and fear that it would isolate me forever. One day last year, my wonderful physician and mentor asked me what the opposite of anger is, and I realized that it is not

the absence of anger, but rather acceptance, laughter, and joy. I also realized that fear and anger just produce more fear and anger, while acceptance brings connection to God and humanity. For many years I had been praying for God to cure my autism and wondering why God didn't answer my prayer. I realize now it is because I had been praying for the wrong reason. I started to pray for the strength to accept autism and life with joy, laughter, and connection. My prayers have been answered more richly than I could ever have imagined! I still passionately hate autism, but now I love life more than I hate autism.

To move from the trap that is anger and fear into acceptance, laughter, and joy—that is the task of an entire lifetime. It is our deepest and most pressing soul work.

About anger our tradition has very little praise. In the Talmud we are told, "One who breaks his garments in anger, breaks his utensils in anger, or scatters his money in anger should appear to you as one who is performing idolatry, for anger is the craft of the *yetzer ha-ra*, the evil inclination" (Shabbat 105b). In anger we lose control of ourselves; we lose all sense of perspective, all direction in life. We lose the ability to savor what is most truly ours. The *Tzava'at ha-Rivash*, a letter of advice attributed to the Ba'al Shem Tov, observes, "When tempted by anger, which is an expression of sinful fear and derives from the attribute of *Gevurah,* overpower your *yetzer* and transform that trait into a chariot of God."

What does it mean to "transform anger into a chariot for God"? It means to so master and transform that emotion that it can serve as a vessel to contain the Holy. It means that through what was previously anger, we now have a portal to the world, that we are able to soar because of the energy liberated from the place the anger had formerly occupied. So, too, with the emotion of fear: the Talmud points out, "However strong the body, fear will break it" (Bava Batra 10a). Our task is to transform fear and anger into a chariot for God—a vehicle capable of shining God's light in the world. To be able to transform these crippling emotions, which trap us under the pretense of allowing us to express our deepest feelings, releases deep wells of resilience, renewal, and hope. It may be tempting to indulge a sense of being made a victim by whatever it is that has victimized us, to wallow in the injustice of whatever has been imposed upon us. Fear and anger, however tempting, are the expression of the *yetzer ha-ra*. They trap and they isolate. And in their wake erupts a tidal wave of crippling rage that incapacitates productive life. It doesn't have to be that way. The Baal Shem Tov says in section 132 of his *Tzava'at ha-Rivash*: "Anger departs with the advent of joy and love."

Can we work—all of us—to focus on cultivating acceptance, joy, and laughter, instead of seeking out yet more things to put on our list of victimhood (How we have been put upon! How we have been misunderstood! How we have been ignored!)? Can we allow the joy that we bring into each other's life to so fill us with delight that all we can do once again is laugh and dance? In our learning, our loving, our challenges, and our chores, can we recognize that we have been given inconceivable blessings, remarkable gifts?

## Little Miracles

I am not going to harp on the reality that, relative to most of humanity, now and throughout time, we are incomparably rich. We are richer than royalty. I won't even insult your intelligence by talking about how the degree of physical security and safety we have is unparalleled. Or remind you how rare a privilege it is that we live in places of political freedom in which we can express our opinion and that we live in an age in which the Jewish people once again enjoy sovereignty in Jerusalem and Zion. I won't speak to you of those mega-blessings. But I would like to direct your attention to the "little" miracles—the fact that the sun is shining, that we have shared a meal, that we are able to learn together, that we have the blessings of community and the blessings of life, and that these gifts ought to be sufficient to inspire in us life-affirming responses. The eighteenth-century transcendentalist poet William Ellery Channing expressed it in these often cited words:

*To live content with small means,*
*to seek elegance rather than luxury,*
*and refinement rather than fashion,*
*to be worthy, not respectable, and wealthy, not rich,*
*to study hard, think quietly, talk gently, act frankly,*
*to listen to stars and birds, babes and sages, with open heart,*
*to bear all cheerfully,*
*do all bravely,*
*await occasions,*
*hurry never—*
*in a word, to let the spiritual, unbidden and unconscious,*
*grow up through the common.*
*This is to be my symphony.*

Our challenge, like Abraham's, is to live our lives as a symphony we conduct; to be able to accept the commonplace and see in it the sacred; like Isaac, to be able to enjoy each moment as an encounter with the Divine, and each person as God's messenger. The Torah commends joy as the pinnacle of divine service: "You are to rejoice before the Holy One" (Deuteronomy 12:18). In commenting on another verse in Deuteronomy that explicates the observance of God's commandment to rejoice, the Mishnah sees two complementary facets of joy: "I have done as you have asked—I have rejoiced and I have caused others to rejoice" (Ma'aser Sheni 5:12). This joy is not narcissism; it is not about self-focus, nor about ignoring human suffering. This sacred joy is the tool for making oneself into a chariot for God. This is about radical celebration, a joy that overpowers injustice and blows away suffering, embracing the wounded, healing the sick, and pursuing *shalom* in its fullest meaning of wholeness. The Zohar tells us that such joy changes multiple worlds, not merely our own:

> The world below is always in a state of receiving, and the upper worlds give to it in accordance with its condition. If it is with radiating countenance, they will be radiant to it in kind from on high;

if it is in a state of sadness, it is given judgment in kind. Thus is it written: "Serve God with joy," for the joy of a person draws forth another joy, a supernal one. (II:184a)

As we are agents of the Divine in the world, eruptions of God's consciousness within Creation, so our joy expresses divine joy and shapes the cosmos. Our ability to rejoice, I have been taught by my teacher, Rabbi Simon Greenberg, is not a matter of happenstance, nor is it the result of what occurs outside of ourself. It is an inner determination to inhabit a place of abiding joy: the joy of *mitzvot*; the joy of community, friends, and family; the joy of life; the joy of being God's child.

May we find the inner strength to move from anger and fear to the shining radiance of acceptance and joy, and in the words of the Talmud, "May the One who gives life to the living grant you a life that is long, and good, and sweet" (Yoma 71a).

# Mindfulness

## Of Children and the Spiritual Life

My children are now adults, moving independently in the world, and I'm learning how to redefine my role as Abba (father) in new ways. But I have been forever transformed by their infancy and the bonds that babies and infants inspire in life-altering and abiding ways. I'm finding God, still, not in the big miracles, but even more so in the little things. Rather than cultivating visions of seas splitting or of mountains leaping like lambs, rather than straining for spiritual ascents to the seventh heaven, I'm discovering the sacred in the constant interruptions and distractions of being alive, of being a father. Just as Abraham's journey with his son Isaac culminated in a mountaintop experience that changed them forever, my children have given me, and continue to give me, the gift of the present.

This awareness of the holiness of the moment isn't my discovery alone. The Buddhists call it "mindfulness," and Jews call it *kavanah*. More an attitude than a skill, this consciousness reflects a focus on living in the world, emerging from the confluence of thought and life experience. When you focus on what you are doing or saying at that particular moment, you demonstrate *kavanah*. I have two adult children, but even when they were little, they both constrained and cultivated a focus I didn't previously possess; they taught me to give up my plans, they forced me to let myself simply be. They shaped and continue to nurture my *kavanah*. When I think of their impact, I picture the Torah's portrayal of Abraham and Isaac on the road to Mount Moriah. We know that Abraham arises early in the morning, saddles the donkeys, packs their bags. We can picture him awakening his son and urging him on as they start to march toward an unknown destination and an unthinkable destiny. For three days, they walk together almost in complete silence.

It is tempting to read that silence as strained and even angry, with each man isolated by his own thoughts and buffeted by his own emotions. Yet the Torah intrudes, not once, but twice, to preclude that understanding:

> Abraham took the wood of the offering and placed it on Isaac, his son. And he took in his hand the flame and the knife; and the two walked together. (Genesis 22:6)

After a brief exchange about God providing the burnt offering, one that sounds prophetic, since we know that God will indeed provide a sheep for the offering, the Torah reiterates that their unity is still robust: "And the two walked together" (Genesis 22:8).

Why, the Rabbis inquire, is this curious observation repeated twice? Rashi understands that the Torah is conveying that Abraham "was going with the same eagerness and joy as Isaac" (Genesis 22:8). The two of them are connected, soul to soul. His experiences with Isaac touch Abraham with a double profundity—as a father and as one who understands his son's perspective—and changes Abraham forever.

## God of Little Children

Prior to having children, my spiritual life was primarily one of sacred Scriptures and prayer. On Shabbat, before going to synagogue, I would wake up early so I could study Talmud for a few hours. When I prayed, I would try to meditate or read some poetry first, to get in the right mood. Sometime during each day, I tried to make time for an hour or two to read and to learn. Of course, since there were no children around, the house was always appropriately quiet for contemplation or for study. Interruptions were rare.

Such an orientation bore rich fruit: my inner life was a bouquet of devotion and connection, what the mystics call *hitboddedut*, of uniting with the Holy One. Solitude and persistence are the requirements of an inner spirituality; productivity and accomplishment are its results. Tranquility and leisurely thought offered untrammeled room for spiritual growth and exploration. I was graced in abundance.

Once the twins grew to infancy, I looked at that previous inner spirituality as through a veil: there was now precious little alone time and far fewer completed tasks. The quiet was gone, and I had no spare moments. I didn't set my alarm anymore; instead, I was awakened (early) by my children. The day offered a series of hurdles: endless needs to be met, and those needs weren't my own. As a result, I didn't have the time to sit down to read a book or to meditate on the marvel of life. Does that mean my spiritual life atrophied? Does this busyness and responsiveness mean I couldn't connect to the Sacred? While my contemplative form of spirituality may have been in abeyance, I discovered—to my surprise—another spiritual form to take its place.

Instead of an inner listening, a meditative stance, mine became an engaged spirituality, a wrestling with little creatures who revealed themselves to be angels if I but showed sufficient tenacity. Just as Abraham only heard God's abiding message after the strenuous effort of arriving at Mount Moriah, only after binding his son and lifting that knife, if I held on long enough, I, too, became witness to the flowering of God's latest miracles: consciousness blossoms, speech finds a surer footing, character consolidates.

## Answering the Call

Our children call, and we must answer. We are obligated to our children—true enough. But the compulsion comes from a place deep within. "*Nafsho keshurah ve-nafsho*—His soul was bound up in his soul," says the Torah about Jacob and his son Benjamin (Genesis 44:30). Our children are a part of us, and we are in exile without them. Our souls yearn for our children the way the medievals pined for Jerusalem. Our *galut* (exile) is their absence. In their presence, surrounded by their noise, chaos, and demands, we feel grounded. That is where we are supposed to be. They are our homeland; they are the footsteps of Messiah.

Which means that my spiritual life was overturned completely. Silence is no longer haven; it is death. Israel is no longer a distant land; it is embodied in these two forms. The ancient God—of Abraham, Isaac, and Jacob—is now my God, the God of Shira and Jacob. My children—even now as adults—call, and through them, I am called. To be a parent, like being a Jew, means having a willingness to live life in the light of that call: Someone wants me. Do I dare respond?

## *Kavanah* of Kids

Before there were children, I bound my tefillin alone. At an early stage of their lives, my four-year-olds would scamper into their Abba's study, take my tefillin bag and insist on "helping" me put them on. Once I was properly garbed, they then would want to *daven* with me, shuckling back and forth as I do. After a few minutes, bored, they began to play in my study, while I, praying above them, no longer would fight their energy, their chaos, and their din. Instead of fearing their uncontainable energy as disruption, I accepted it as God's bounty—a limitless divine effusion of love, of health, and of life. My *kavanah* no longer focused on the words in the siddur, but on the confluence of ancient words of praise and boundless childish enthusiasm. This, too, was an encounter with God: unrehearsed, raw, imposing.

A popular contemporary proverb holds that "life is what happens while we are making plans." I now know that God erupts in the guise of life, sheer exuberance, untrained zest, smiles, drippy noses, tears. Formless and endless, children are the vessels through which godliness becomes visible even to contriving adults. Our children were, and are the still, small voice. Our children summon us to put down our plans, set aside our studies, attend, and live.

In a remarkable insight into the binding of Isaac, one commentator noticed that Abraham had to be called twice. Having walked for three days, climbed the mountain, bound his son, and raised the knife, Abraham was no longer in the moment, no longer attentive to the world around him. Rabbi Moses Alshich, sixteenth-century Kabbalist of Tzfat, remarks that Abraham was so determined to carry out the commandment that he did not listen to the new voice, the intrusion bidding him to refrain from the sacrifice of his son. He needed to be called twice in order to desist (*Torat Mosheh*, commentary to Genesis 22:11).

It is in the openness to distractions and interruptions that God is to be found. In the moment, open to what may come—bruised knees or a child at play—we live. And our studies, our *mitzvot*, our communities—they train us to be able to look, to focus our mindfulness, and to see God in our children's smiles, to hear God in their squeals and shrieks. They alert us, like a map to divine terrain, of where the journey may lead, if we will only show a willingness to stay the course and to follow our worthy guides: our children.

# Suffering

## A New Jewish Response

The topics of theodicy (literally, "God's justice") and eschatology ("discussion of the end-time") are probably the most severe challenges to religious faith in general and to liberal religion in particular. They challenge religious faith in that theodicy is an attempt to explain the presence, indeed the pervasiveness, of evil in a world created by God. How, using our example, could a loving God command Abraham to sacrifice his beloved and innocent son? How could the same God who promised Abraham an eternal covenant through Isaac be the one to demand his death at the hands of that righteous and innocent father?

Our very language, *an attempt to explain*, highlights the fact that the existence of that evil is a serious problem—a powerful impediment to the belief in a loving and powerful God. Liberal faith is particularly challenged because it does not have the comfort, however illusory, of a literally revealed Truth to rely on. We are forced to stumble in the haze, using a combination of reason, intuition, tradition, and emotion to establish a path through the pain. In that integrated understanding, the story of the *Akedah* becomes the focal point for our anguish, a telling that captures our sense of living in a world in which we must often sacrifice what we most cherish. We know that we must move forward, but we aren't sure which way forward really is.

Our challenge: evil does exist in the world, and it exists in abundance. It strikes at the great and the obscure, the moral and the vile, the young and the old with arbitrary indifference. The existence of goodness and morality may pose a problem for the atheist's philosophy; the existence of this immoral/amoral evil is certainly a problem for a believer's understanding. How could a God worth worshiping possibly abide by, let alone create, so much suffering? Certainly the events of the *Akedah* raise that question, as God not only allows but intentionally creates the grounding for Abraham's anguish.

For traditional monotheists (those who construe God as having no less personality than God's Creation), looking on a broader scale, the issue is as painful and clear: How could a good God allow all this suffering? But the issue is no less intense for those who construe God using metaphors of an impersonal force: How does that force lead to a triumph of well-being over suffering? How does it provide comfort—physical or spiritual—during times of tribulation? Are the outbursts of suffering the consequence of other, more malignant, forces (a.k.a. gods)?

## Social Evil versus Natural Evil

Let us, for the sake of clarity, sharpen our distinction. There exists two broad categories of evil—social evil and natural evil. Social evil (the severe disparities of wealth and opportunities between different individuals or between different societies: the Holocaust, food shortages, sexism, racism, homophobia) can be attributed to the essential nature of human freedom and free will. Unless people are to be moral automatons, some will clearly exercise the option to make the wrong choices—some people will pursue their own interests at the expense of other people, some will lust for power, for vengeance, for violence. For God to prevent those choices is to reduce human beings to moral robots. Social evil is the price we pay for autonomy. (We can still ask why, in an infinite range of possible universes, God had to make one in which those extremes are the only two choices.)

So, relatively speaking, social evil need not pose a severe challenge to religious faith. Not so, however, with natural evil. There is no moral reason why viruses should be able to make people's dying years so miserable, why instant crib death should exist, why some people are unable to walk or see or hear. Here there is no issue of moral autonomy at stake—we see only meaninglessness and undeserved suffering. I have no answer to instant crib death. There is a hole in my faith.

## How to Respond to Suffering

The range of attempted responses to this problem are as wide as they are ineffective. "We are punished for our sins" does not help at the funeral of a child. Being "purged now so we can be rewarded later" doesn't address the question of why a loving God would require suffering at all. That "the universe is structured to permit moral growth" dodges the issue of why that structure isn't more constantly clear and why it should require innocent agony.

I admit from the outset that I do not have an adequate theological response to natural evil. But I do have a strong sense of what such a response must entail.

The first guideline must be the recognition that evil is real. There are outlooks and faiths that deny or disparage the fact of evil. This is, I believe, callous and self-centered. People perceive pain. Watching a man who is in the last stages of terminal illness and telling him that pain is merely a figment of his sinful imagination, simply the absence or distance of God, is cruel and abusive. Such a theology is unworthy of moral people or of a loving God. So rule number one is that evil is real and must be dealt with as a reality.

Rule number two is that the theology must be one that would be helpful to a person in pain. Far too often, we develop complex theologies that would either reveal their inadequacy or compound the sufferer's pain were we to dare to suggest these theological responses to people who are suffering. Were we to tell a mourner about "*mipnei hata'enu galinu*—we were exiled because of our sins," we would be ashamed. Our theology must not be shameful, and it must not need to be restricted to seminaries and theology workshops. It must bring comfort when comfort is needed and where pain is felt.

The third guideline is that the theology must build on elements found within the Jewish heritage. Accepting the postulate that religion is not merely an intellectual exercise, particularly at moments of anguish, it is crucial that Jewish symbols, stories, and rituals be reintegrated so as to lend their strength and subconscious resonance to the person in pain. Abraham's response is not one of intellectual distance. Nor does he respond by minimizing his own sorrow and Isaac's terror. Indeed, we are told that it is objectively tragic: "When the patriarch Abraham stretched forth his hand to take the knife to slay his son, the angels wept" (*Bereshit Rabbah* 56:5). Nonetheless, Abraham says, "*Hineni*—Here I am," evincing an existential willingness to live in whatever comes, to experience fully, to respond as himself to the pain and the suffering no less than to the joys and triumphs.

The path that I believe integrates these three points most effectively is a modern reintegration of Kabbalah as found in Process Thought, a philosophical approach that understands all creation (and the Creator) as dynamic, interrelated, and self-determining at every level. According to this schema, somehow God suffers when we do, God is in need of human mending and able to contribute to human emotional and spiritual empowerment, and Shekhinah is always accessible to human relation. These are the elements from which a new Jewish response to pain might emerge.

By refusing to abandon hope in the face of bleak reality, by refusing to wish away a challenging reality in favor of simplistic beliefs and wishful stories, Abraham remains true to the *brit*, the covenant. Such a notion recognizes that pain is an ever-present reality in our world—but a reality that God and humanity can oppose together. It mobilizes the power of sacred story and of community in the battle against meaninglessness and isolation. And it teaches that, ultimately, we will repair the breach—God, the world, and humanity will one day be whole.

# CONCLUSION

# Belief—Know Before Whom You Stand

U ntil now, the tests we have examined were tests of the towering figures within the story itself: Abraham, Isaac, Sarah, even God. But this last, final test is our own. In light of life's challenges, our own beliefs are sorely tested. We find ourselves tried by our experiences, by events in the world at large. And we find ourselves bound to the altar of clashing principles, hurtful relationships, communal challenges. How, amid our own trial and binding, can we affirm our own beliefs? How can we turn to the universe in expectation and hope? How can we continue to work toward a better tomorrow?

Let us be clear: this last test may well be found by responding to a story in the Torah, but that story is merely the avatar for life in the world as a whole. Our theological reflection must bring us back to life as it's lived, must inspire us to live life better and to affirm hope more resiliently, and must gird us to fight more passionately for justice, compassion, and love.

Our journey begins in life. We arm ourselves with ideas, practices, and traditions, and then we must return to life. Reflection is a middle step, a tool along the way. It is vital and empowering, but it remains the middle step on a much longer path. And it is not the goal. The goal is life.

## Can We Face Our Own Test?

Much of contemporary theological exchange is marred by the coerciveness of its participants. Few people discuss theology in order to account for the broadest number of facts and perceptions. Instead, theology is often characterized by a twofold attempt to coerce others to believe the way the theologian does and to compare the selected best of one's own tradition against the less (subjectively) palatable aspects of another's. Both efforts prevent us from understanding other people's perceptions of the world and inhibit our own religious growth. I wish to avoid both flaws.

So, at the outset, I must confess that I have no desire to persuade others to believe in God the way I do or for the reasons I do. I offer my own perceptions of God, hoping that you will do the same and that through our mutual attempts to internalize or even to reject (after careful thought) each other's theology, we will emerge somewhat wiser, more sophisticated, and better servants of God.

I have an additional confession to make. While I consider myself part of the broad coalition of Process thinkers, I continue to glean insights and wisdom from diverse and incompatible approaches to philosophy and theology. To reduce God to one philosophical system (ontological, experiential, or existential) is to miss the full extent of God's majesty. This reduction is no less belittling to God than is the attempt to claim that God's complete revelation can be contained in mere words. This caveat is not intended as an excuse for sloppy thinking or unjustifiable conclusions, simply to assert that we experience God on many levels, that people are complex creatures, and that any theology that ignores that multifacetedness and that complexity cannot do justice to its subject.

Living as a Jew, I spend a good deal of time in a synagogue and read the *parashah* every week. Living in southern California, my family and I are frequent visitors to Disneyland. When they were children, Jacob and Shira, my wife, and I especially loved the section called "Toontown," the neighborhood of some of Disneyland's most

famous celebrities. Here it is possible to actually see the home of Min-
nie Mouse, as well as to meet her. Even more thrilling is the home of
her lifelong companion, Mickey, just next door.

After touring each room of the house, examining Mickey's reading chair, television, and washing machine, we are finally led to
Mickey's private theater, where his classic films are showing. Visitors
wait there so they can be ushered into Mickey's presence in small
numbers, allowing greater intimacy when the anticipated moment
comes. Finally, when our turn arrives, we are led down a corridor, a
door opens, and there he is. I will never forget how Jacob, my then–
two-year-old son, ran to Mickey's feet and wouldn't let go. The look
on his face was one of complete rapture, and I have never seen him
happier or more absorbed.

## The Religious Issue at Stake

I am a rabbi, and my life is devoted to the service of God and Torah,
which means that everything I do gets filtered through the peculiar
lenses of my ancient craft. Jacob's enchantment in the presence of this
cartoon character led me to think about the power of imagination and
the truths it can access. What is it about the human mind that leads us
to imagine beings we cannot see, creatures of our own fantasies, and
then to love them with such overpowering force? Children are simply
the most visible practitioners of loving their own imagined images.
But we all do it—we know that Romeo and Juliet is a fantasy, yet we
cry at the lovers' demise; we watch *Casablanca* (for the thousandth
time yet!) and are deeply touched by Rick's selfless love. Having made
it this far in this book, you have spent a significant amount of time
walking with Abraham and Isaac and, along the way, dwelling with
Sarah in her tent. Something about the way people are built impels us
to create stories and invent characters who then are allowed entry into
the most private chambers of our souls. We rejoice at their triumphs
and their ingenuity, we mourn their tragedies and failings, all the
while aware that they "exist" only as a product of our creative energy.

What can we learn from our drive to imagine? What does our need to empathize with fictional figures tell us about ourselves and about the world? What does my son's passion for Mickey Mouse reveal about the human condition?

The reason this issue is particularly pressing to me is that I am a lover of God. Fully aware that God has been portrayed in a staggering variety of ways throughout the ages and across diverse traditions, I know that my own inner response to God is not very different from my son's response to a Disney cartoon. Understanding Jacob's relationship to Mickey Mouse can help us to formulate a clearer notion of how we relate to God and just what that relationship entails.

Of course, classical analytical interpretation would assert that this love of Mickey Mouse (or of God) is simply a delusion, an inner projection of our own insecurities and the need to be sheltered by some external fallacy. There is no Mickey Mouse, but our fears of finitude, helplessness, and abandonment impel us to create these falsehoods to gain an artificial sense of security. We coat a harsh world in the gentle blanket of a lie. The lie may be serviceable in the short term—it does make the universe less frightening. But in the long term, this fantasy, like all falsehoods, is crippling, requiring more and more psychic energy to maintain in the face of life's harsh disappointments and cruel reality. The key to health, in this worldview, is to face the world unadorned, to move beyond the reliance on myths, however comforting or venerable. Mickey Mouse, to this school of thought, is no different than God. Just as we expect a child to outgrow the cartoon, so, too, a healthy adult ought to transcend the Transcendent.

There is a great deal of power and coherence in this explanation of fantasy, and it reflects a direct challenge to the entire enterprise of religion—both in its fundamentalist and its more liberal modes. Seeking solace, order, and purpose through faith and ritual, regardless of whether the sacred stories are understood as historically true or as metaphorically true, is simple delusion, a pathology to eradicate. Religion, for Freud and his classical followers, is the enemy. And so is Mickey Mouse.

## Is Mickey Mouse the Enemy? Is God?

There are some problems with Freud's confident dismissal of religion as delusion, not least of which is the testimony of religious people throughout the ages who associate their faith with great joy, resilience, and profundity. Abraham's faith carries him through agonizing days of silence and redeems him in the end. Isaac uses faith to offer the ultimate sacrifice. Even in our age of technological sophistication and scientific skepticism, religious faith continues to exercise a tremendous attraction, transcending all educational and financial divisions. Indeed, even among psychoanalysts there is a strong representation of the faithful, forcing a reevaluation of what religion represents even within the field that Freud built.

Indeed, we needn't look so far for the positive role of faith. Merely look, with me, at my son's joyous glee in the presence of his beloved mouse. Mickey allows him to connect with the world, to feel a sense of belonging and of reciprocal caring that deepens his humanity and makes him feel more alive. Mickey is clearly a force for good in his life, just as God is for the billions who believe.

But whether or not something "works" does not confirm its veracity. We can use the belief that the earth is flat to calm an irrational fear of falling off, but the functionality of a claim doesn't make it true. As a rabbi and a seeking Jew, I'm not willing to devote my life to something that functions through a lie. I don't want a mere delusion of holiness to help build community. I want God to be real.

In what way, then, is God real?

## The Reality of Mickey Mouse

In considering the ways in which God is real, Mickey Mouse can provide some insight, too.

When a child falls in love with Mickey Mouse, what the child loves is the caring, warm, and joyous image that Mickey represents. In the sense of being a discrete character, Mickey doesn't really exist. But in the sense of embodying certain values and characteristics, what Mickey represents is very real indeed. Mickey is merely one possible representation of that reality. There is no way to give unmediated form to love and fidelity, but it is possible to cloak those virtues in the garment of a character or the vehicle of a story. Love can never appear in the abstract: it must always be a specific love that is felt by someone for someone or something else. So, too, faith, hope, or truth.

Fantasy, it seems, is how human beings make visible the invisible realities of life. Not less real, but more so, these intangible passions and commitments are at the very core of life, making life worth living and society possible. Without the versimilitude of fiction and art, we wouldn't be able to transmit or articulate the realities that undergird meaningful living. Fantasy gives us access to the most significant truths—loyalty, compassion, morality, passion, and trust. The story of Abraham's trial need not have been a specific historical event for it to convey life-enhancing truths. What Jacob responds to in Mickey Mouse is absolutely true and is embodied in that cartoon character, even as it transcends Mickey's limits. The cartoon doesn't have an independent existence, but what it points to does, and is more real than most of the tangible delusions people glorify and pursue.

## God as a Cosmic Mickey Mouse

God has a lot in common with Mickey Mouse, representing the part of reality that eludes measurement or analysis, but that makes life worthwhile. What we learn from Mickey Mouse is that the character is the embodiment of a reality that ultimately eludes us. God, too, is the concrete image of values and truths that can never be fully articulated or represented. But where God differs from Mickey Mouse is that God is not only the metaphor that makes those virtues visible to us, but the deeper reality itself. As thirteenth-century Jewish philosopher Moses Maimonides notes so presciently, "God is the knower, the subject of knowledge, and the knowledge itself—all in one" (*Mishneh Torah, Hilkhot Yesodei ha-Torah* 2:10).

If the virtues and truths that God represents are impossible to contain, then ultimately it is impossible to speak about God in any literally meaningful way. God is not some tangible truth to be dissected, scrutinized, or analyzed. Just as we cannot explain what love feels like to someone who has never felt it, it is impossible to talk about God. We can only affirm God. Similarly, we use language to allude to a particular emotion, hoping to provide enough guidance and signposts so the listener can more successfully experience love itself. Love cannot be described once and for all; it can only be alluded to and celebrated. Perhaps that's why the greatest words about love are found in poetry, which attempts to evoke, rather than to inform. All God talk is ultimately poetry.

Just as poems use different metaphors to describe the same emotion or virtue, so, too, can religion employ different images to describe the same transcendent unity that we call God. The Rabbis recognize this irreducible theological pluralism when they write that "God is like an icon that never changes, yet everyone who looks into it sees a different face" (*Pesikta de-Rav Kahana* 110a). Or yet again when they relate that "God was revealed at the Red Sea as a hero waging war, and at Sinai as an elder full of compassion, ... [yet] it is the same God in Egypt, the same God at the Red Sea, the same God in the past, the same God in the future" (*Mekhilta, Shirata, Beshallah* 4). The reality that our perception points to is always greater than our ability to express in words. The very limitations of our own finite perspective, our cultural embeddedness, and our personal histories profoundly shape how we see and relate to that underlying reality. Perhaps the greatest biblical theologian, then, is Hagar (Sarah's maidservant, whom Sarah offered to Abraham when she was unable to produce a child, and with whom Abraham fathered Ishmael), who recognized that how she knew God was a reflection of her own vision: "And she [Hagar] called the Holy One who spoke to her, 'God of My Seeing'" (Genesis 16:13).

How we see God is all we can talk about. It's the outer garment that religion uses to attempt to communicate what can only be experienced directly. God is perceived "according to the power of each individual, according to the individual power of the young, the old, and the very small ones" (*Shemot Rabbah* 29:1). Just as Mickey Mouse is an embodiment of certain wonderful emotions and values that can only make their appearance in the form of specific characters, so the values that God embodies—holiness, righteousness, wisdom, and compassion—can only be made tangible through specific religious forms. The tests we face in life can be faced through the telling of the tale of the binding of Isaac, and we can better confront our own trials by recounting and empathizing with that of Abraham.

Each religion, then, offers a culturally based filter to make those timeless truths apparent to its believers. Since we can only be receptive to something that speaks our own language, the task of each religious tradition is to intuit these cosmic human profundities and to garb them in the clothing of speech. "The Torah speaks in human language" (Talmud, Yevamot 71a), the Rabbis assert, because otherwise we would be incapable of hearing its wisdom or responding to the cosmos.

So God is, at one level, a culturally bound metaphor. Inescapably, since we must rely on language to communicate, and language (including art) always develops among a concrete community sharing a particular history, how we speak of the Sacred and the good will assume contextual form—through the stories, rituals, and prayers of our own faith traditions. As the Zohar recognizes, "All this is said only from our point of view, and it is relative to our knowledge" (II:176a). Like Abraham, our *Hineni* means we stand in a specific time and place, as distinct and specific individuals who compose particular communities. There is no other way to talk, and no other perch from which to respond.

Yet the matter doesn't end there. These expressions of elusive truths do point to something real, something that each human being experiences with overwhelming power. During those peak moments in our lives—when we are married, at the birth of a child, or the death of a loved one—that inexpressible reality is so real that all else pales in its presence. That our descriptions of God are culturally bound cannot eclipse the God beyond the metaphors, the Holy One to whom those metaphors point. Even while recognizing that the perception of God is "according to the power of each individual," that same midrash asserts, "Do not believe that there are many deities in heaven because you have heard many voices, but know that I alone am the Holy One your God" (*Shemot Rabbah* 29:1).

For there are eternal verities that have enriched life through the ages. There are grand truths and values more wondrous than life itself that lift us up and strengthen our resolve. Our metaphors, the way we speak about God, help to remind us of the truths buried deep in our hearts and shining at us from the brightest stars. Judged from this perspective, the tale of Isaac's binding—and religion as a whole—is true when it helps us to shape our lives by those timeless profundities and helps us to experience those elevating sentiments. Religion works when it plugs us into the reality of being connected with all that is and all that ever was, when it infuses our lives with purpose and our communities with a zeal for justice and compassion. Religion is true, in short, when it can produce godliness among its practitioners, justice among its disciples, and a deep sense of belonging and peace. Surely the great tales of the Torah are true in that sense, and the way of life found in its *mitzvot* paves a pathway of peace.

As Rabbi Abraham Joshua Heschel notes, "A Jew is asked to take a leap of action rather than a leap of thought; to surpass his needs, to do more than he understands in order to understand more than he does" (*God in Search of Man*, 283). We demonstrate the validity of our understanding of God—its power to serve as a vehicle for truths otherwise inexpressible yet profoundly real—by the way we live our lives, by the way we fashion a sacred community, by the way we are true to our ancient covenant. "There is no Monarch without a nation"(*Commentary to the Torah, Parashat Va-Yera*), the medieval Jewish philosopher Bahya ben Asher admitted. We make our God (as metaphor) reflect God (the reality) by our willingness to live as God's people, by our willingness to make the values and *mitzvot* of Judaism live through our deeds. Perhaps that's what we mean when we say the *Shema*: Adonai, our understanding of God, is ultimately a reflection of the *Ein Sof*, the One beyond all description.

And that is no Mickey Mouse.

# Acknowledgments

As with the writing of any book, there are many people to thank. This book owes much to the good people who gave it their careful attention. I am particularly grateful to those who read drafts of the work in progress.

Thanks to my friend Stuart M. Matlins, founder and publisher of Jewish Lights; Emily Wichland, editor extraordinaire; Kaitlin Johnstone, masterful editor and coach; Jennifer Rataj and Kelly O'Neill, skilled publicists; and the talented people at Jewish Lights, who accepted an unfinished manuscript and produced a beautiful and significantly better book.

While writing this book, it has been my delight to serve as the Abner and Roslyn Goldstein Dean of the Ziegler School of Rabbinic Studies and vice president of American Jewish University in Los Angeles. I am reminded daily of the blessing of working with an outstanding group of people: students, faculty, administration, and lay leaders. My deepest thanks go to the university's president, Dr. Robert Wexler, who is both mentor and friend; to Rabbi Cheryl Peretz, Rabbi Aaron Alexander, and Reb Mimi Feigelson—partners in building a world-class rabbinical school in the context of holiness, goodness, and friendship; to the superb members of the faculty; and to my beloved students—rabbis and soon-to-be rabbis. It is a privilege and a joy to work at such a wonderful *makom Torah* (place of Torah).

My continuing thanks and affection also go to the Jewish Theological Seminary, where I was ordained as a rabbi and where I still cherish friendships and many close ties, and to the Hebrew Union College–Jewish Institute of Religion, where I was granted the privilege of doctoral studies under the scholarly and humane supervision of my teacher and friend, Rabbi David Ellenson.

Of course, my beloved family has provided a constant backdrop of love and support. I am deeply grateful to my mother, Barbara Friedman Artson, and her companion, Richard Lichtman; my father, David Artson, and his wife, Jeanne; my sister and sister-in-law, Tracy and Dawn Osterweil-Artson; my niece, Sydney, and my nephew, Benjamin; my brother, Matthew Artson; and Grace Mayeda, my beloved childhood nanny.

I have been privileged to have many wonderful rabbis and spiritual guides enrich my life—too many to list—and I am grateful to each and every one of them. But I do want to use this book to celebrate one great teacher, Rabbi Simon Greenberg, who took me under his wing while I was in rabbinical school and shared with me his love of the Torah, the book of Psalms, Abraham Lincoln, brisk walks, Israel, married life, *mitzvot*, a water-clear integrity, and a lifelong passion for learning and rectitude. My first sermon on the *Akedah* was honed under his watchful gaze, and I think of him often and with love.

My children, Jacob and Shira, fill my life with profound joy and purpose. While it may seem that they have required some sacrifices here and there, the rewards of seeing them grow into such kind, compassionate, and decent people is purest delight. And to see them emerging into their own fills me with joy and makes me eager to savor their future flowering.

My beloved wife, Elana, is my partner as we journey together toward that unnamed destination. To have the privilege of sharing my life with my lifelong best friend is a true privilege and an abiding joy. She is indefatigable on behalf of our children and our family and has taught me more about the strength of living fully than anyone.

To the memory of Rabbi Simon Greenberg, and to my beloved Elana, Shira, and Jacob, I lovingly dedicate this book.

*Aharon aharon haviv*—I am grateful beyond words to the Holy Blessing One. You have allowed me the privilege of studying, teaching, and observing Your Torah, of glimpsing, from time to time, the shimmering light, and of rejoicing to mold the warmth of that light into words. I pray that this book will in some small way refract Your divine love and allow others to grow with Your word.

My blessing for us all is found in ancient words, "May the One who answered Abraham on Mount Moriah answer you and hearken this day to the sound of your cry."

*Tam venishlam shevach le-el borei olam.*

# Notes

1. Rebecca Goldstein, *The Mind-Body Problem,* (New York: Penguin, 1993), 25.

2. "How to Look at Torah," *Zohar: The Book of Enlightenment* (New York: Paulist Press, 1983), 43–44, 3:152a.

3. Barry D. Walfish, "Medieval Jewish Interpretation," *The Jewish Study Bible*, Adele Berlin and Marc Zvi Brettler, eds. (Oxford, UK: Oxford University Press, 2004), 1893.

4. Michael Fishbane, "Hermeneutics," in *Contemporary Jewish Religious Thought*, Arthur A. Cohen and Paul Mendes-Flohr, eds. (New York: Charles Scribner's Sons, 1987), 359.

# Glossary

**Adonai:** The word read aloud instead of the Tetragrammaton, the four-letter name of God. Often translated as "the LORD."

**Akedah:** The Hebrew term for "binding." Short for the binding of Isaac.

**Akedat Yitzhak:** The Hebrew term for "the binding of Isaac."

**Avimelekh:** King of Gerar, mentioned several times in the book of Genesis.

**Avot de-Rabbi Natan:** Talmudic commentary to Pirkei Avot.

**Ba-Midbar Rabbah:** A standardized collection of Rabbinic Midrash dealing with the verses of the Book of Numbers in sequential form.

**Beit Ha-Mikdash:** The Holy Temple in Israel, and Judaism's most sacred site. The First Temple was built by King Solomon in the year 1000 BCE, and the Second Temple was built by Ezra and Nehemiah in 513 BCE.

**Bereshit Rabbah:** Early Rabbinic Midrash to Genesis.

**Brit:** The Hebrew term for "covenant."

**Davar:** The Hebrew term for "word" or "thing."

**Daven:** Yiddish meaning "to pray."

**Derash:** The Hebrew term for commentary. One of the four levels of commentary, focusing on the ethical and religious message.

**Eid ul-Adha:** Muslim festival commemorating the trial of Abraham.

**Ein Sof:** That aspect of God that is beyond all knowing, description, or relationship. God as infinite and without limitations or divisons of any kind. In Lurianic Kabbalah, this is often portrayed as above the Sefirot, or in circular form, as surrounding the concentric circles of Sefirot.

**Elohim:** The Hebrew term for "God."

**Emunah:** The Hebrew term for "trust" and "faithfulness."

**Gevurah:** In Kabbalah, one of God's emanations, that of judgment, strength, containment, and limitation.

**Hajj:** The Muslim concept of making pilgrimage to Mecca and Medina.

**Ha-Makom:** A Hebrew term meaning "the place," used for God.

**Hineni:** A Hebrew term meaning "Here I am."

**Hitboddedut:** Hasidic term for mindful focus on being alone with God, even in the midst of a crowd or while performing a task.

**Kabbalah:** A Hebrew term meaning "tradition" or "what is transmitted"; signifies the mystical tradition.

**Kavanah:** Hebrew term for mindfulness, focus, intention.

**Korban:** Sacrifice, from the Hebrew for "to draw near."

**Lekh lekha:** God's command to Abraham, "Go forth," in Genesis 12:1.

**Ma'akhelet:** The large butcher knife used by Abraham in the binding.

**Ma'asim tovim:** Hebrew term for "good deeds."

**Malakh:** Angel, messenger.

**Mekhilta:** The earliest Rabbinic Midrash, dealing with the Book of Exodus.

**Midrash:** Rabbinic commentary to the Bible, either legal or narrative.

**Midrash Va-Yosha:** An ancient Midrash.

**Minchah:** Grain offering in biblical times; became the name for the afternoon prayers.

**Mishnah:** The earliest compilation of Rabbinic law; assembled by Rabbi Judah ha-Nasi around the year 200 CE.

**Mitzvah:** Commandment, later also understood as a good deed.

**Moriah:** The region and mountain of the trial of Abraham. Understood to be the Temple Mount (Mount Zion) in Jerusalem, known in Arabic as *al-aram al-quds ash-sharif*, the Noble Sanctuary.

**Mount Zion:** The Temple Mount in Jerusalem.

**Na:** An adverb indicating polite request, "if you please ..."

**Na'ar:** Youth.

**Nes:** Miracle, test, trial.

**Nisayon:** Trial, test, experience.

**Pardes:** Persian word for "paradise." Also the four-layered approach to biblical commentary.

**Peshat:** Simple. The literal layer of biblical interpretation.

**Pesikta de-Rav Kahana:** A later midrashic collection that deals with the holiday cycle and the annual calendar in sermonic form.

**Pesikta Rabbati:** A medieval collection of Rabbinic Midrashim on the entire Torah, Haftarot, and special Sabbath readings.

**Pirkei Avot:** Collection of Rabbinic aphorisms in the Mishnah, written around the year 250 CE.

**Pseudo-Yonatan:** Aramaic translation and commentary of the Bible.

**Qur'an:** The holiest book of Islam, understood to be Allah's direct revelations to the Prophet Muhammad.

**Rashi:** Rabbi Shlomo Yitzhaki, unparalleled eleventh-century French commentator to the Bible and Talmud.

**Remez:** Hint. One of the four approaches to Bible commentary, accentuating the allegorical and philosophical meanings.

**Rosh Ha-Shanah:** The Jewish New Year.

**Satan:** The Accuser. Not a name, but a title (*ha-Satan*), *ha-Satan* is the prosecutor in God's court.

**Shalom:** Hebrew term for peace, greetings, farewell. Arguably Judaism's capstone value.

**Shekhinah:** God's indwelling presence, immanence. In Kabbalah, viewed as a feminine aspect of the divine, in exile with the people of Israel during the week, and reunited with the masculine aspects of the divine on the Sabbath.

**Shemot Rabbah:** A standardized collection of Rabbinic Midrash dealing with the verses of the Book of Exodus in sequential form.

***Sod*:** Secret, hidden. The mystical layer of biblical interpretation.

**Talmud:** The great Rabbinic compendium of wisdom, law, stories, philosophy, liturgy, agriculture, and commentary, from sixth, century Babylon.

***Talmud Torah:*** The study of Torah.

**Tanakh:** Acronym for the Hebrew Bible [T=*Torah*, N=*Nevi'im* (Prophets), KH=*Khetuvim* (Writings)].

***Tanhuma*:** A later medieval collection of Rabbinic Midrashim on the entire Torah.

**Tetragrammaton:** The ineffable four-letter name of God: Y-H-V-H.

***Tikkum olam*:** Kabbalistic/Hasidic term for repair of the cosmos from its primal rupture. The breaking of vessels containing divine energy. Contemporary use extends this idea into the realm of social justice and social action.

**Torah:** The first five books of the Bible—Genesis, Exodus, Leviticus, Numbers, Deuteronomy.

***Tzedakah*:** Hebrew term that literally means "justice, equality." Has come to have a specialized meaning as "charity."

***Va-Yikra Rabbah*:** A standardized collection of Rabbinic Midrash dealing with the verses of the Book of Leviticus in sequential form.

**Yachid:** Favored one.

**Y-H-V-H:** The Tetragrammaton; see above.

***Yirei Elohim*:** God-fearer.

**Zion:** Israel; see also Mount Zion.

**Zohar:** Core books of Kabbalah, these commentaries to the Torah reveal mystical meanings. Traditionally ascribed to the second-century sage Rabbi Shimon bar Yohai and understood by modern scholars to be the work of Moshe de Leon (fourteenth-century Spanish sage).

# Bibliography

Auerbach, Erich. *Mimesis: The Representation of Reality in Western Literature.* Princeton: Princeton University Press, 1953, p. 15.

Agus, Aharon (Ronald E.). *The Binding of Isaac & Messiah: Law, Martyrdom, and Deliverance in Early Rabbinic Religiosity.* Albany: State University of New York Press, 1988.

Berman, Louis A. *The Akedah: The Binding of Isaac.* Northvale, NJ: Jason Aronson, 1997.

Cohen, Norman J. *Hineini in Our Lives: Learning How to Respond to Others through 14 Biblical Texts & Personal Stories.* Woodstock, VT: Jewish Lights Publishing, 2003.

———. *Masking and Unmasking Ourselves: Interpreting Biblical Texts on Clothing & Identity.* Woodstock, VT: Jewish Lights Publishing, 2012.

———. *Voices from Genesis: Guiding Us through the Stages of Life.* Woodstock, VT: Jewish Lights Publishing, 1998.

Crenshaw, James L. *A Whirlpool of Torment: Israelite Traditions of God as an Oppressive Presence.* Philadelphia: Fortress Press, 1984.

Fox, Marvin. "Kierkegaard and Rabbinic Judaism." *Judaism* (2 April 1953): 160–169. Reprinted in *Marvin Fox Collected Essays on Philosophy and on Judaism.* Volume 2. Jacob Neusner, ed. Binghamton, NY: Global Publications, 2001.

Friedman, Richard Elliot. *Commentary on the Torah.* San Francisco: HarperSanFrancisco, 2001.

———. *The Bible with Sources Revealed.* San Francisco: HarperSanFrancisco, 2003.

Goodman, L. E. *God of Abraham*. New York: Oxford University Press, 1996.

Herschel, Abraham Joshua. *God in Search of Man*. New York: Octagon Books, 1972.

Kaplan, Mordecai. *Meaning of God in Modern Jewish Religion*. Detroit: Wayne State University Press, 1995, p. 68.

Krauss, Pesach. *Why Me? Coping with Grief, Loss and Change*. Toronto: Bantam Books, 1988, p. 51.

Laufer, Nathan. *The Genesis of Leadership: What the Bible Teaches Us about Vision, Values and Leading Change*. Woodstock, VT: Jewish Lights Publishing, 2006.

Lerner, Michael. *Jewish Renewal*. New York: Harper Perennial, 1995.

Levenson, Jon D. *The Death and Resurrection of the Beloved Son: The Transformation of Child Sacrifice in Judaism and Christianity*. New Haven, CT: Yale University Press, 1993.

Milgrom, Jo. *The Binding of Isaac: The Akedah—A Primary Symbol in Jewish Thought and Art*. Berkeley, CA: BIBAL Press, 1988.

Morgenstern, Julian. *A Jewish Interpretation of the Book of Genesis*. Cincinnati: Union of American Hebrew Congregations, 1920, pp. 160–161.

Ridley, Aaron, ed. *Neitzsche: The Anti-Christ, Ecce Homo, Twilight of the Idols and Other Writings*. New York: Cambridge University Press, 2005, p. 157.

Royce, Josiah. *The Philosophy of Loyalty*. New York: The MacMillian Company, 1908.

Rosenzweig, Franz. *Understanding the Sick and Healthy*. New York: The Noonday Press, 1953.

Salkin, Jeffrey K. *Righteous Gentiles in the Hebrew Bible: Ancient Role Models for Sacred Relationships*. Woodstock, VT: Jewish Lights Publishing, 2008.

Sarna, Nahum M. *The JPS Torah Commentary: Genesis*. Philadelphia: Jewish Publication Society, 1989.

Schulweis, Harold M. *Conscience: The Duty to Obey and the Duty to Disobey*. Woodstock, VT: Jewish Lights Publishing, 2008.

Speiser, E. A. *The Anchor Bible: Genesis*. New York: Doubleday, 1982.

Spiegel, Shalom. *The Last Trial: On the Legends and Lore of the Command to Abraham to Offer Isaac as a Sacrifice: The Akedah*. Woodstock, VT: Jewish Lights, 1993.

# AVAILABLE FROM BETTER BOOKSTORES.
# TRY YOUR BOOKSTORE FIRST.

## *Bible Study/Midrash*

**The Book of Job:** Annotated & Explained
*Translation and Annotation by Donald Kraus; Foreword by Dr. Marc Brettler*
Clarifies for today's readers what Job is, how to overcome difficulties in the text, and what it may mean for us. Features fresh translation and probing commentary.
5½ x 8½, 256 pp, Quality PB, 978-1-59473-389-5 **$16.99**

**Masking and Unmasking Ourselves:** Interpreting Biblical Texts on Clothing & Identity  *By Dr. Norman J. Cohen*
Presents ten Bible stories that involve clothing in an essential way, as a means of learning about the text, its characters and their interactions.
6 x 9, 240 pp, HC, 978-1-58023-461-0 **$24.99**

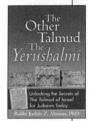

**The Other Talmud—*The Yerushalmi*:** Unlocking the Secrets of The Talmud of Israel for Judaism Today  *By Rabbi Judith Z. Abrams, PhD*
A fascinating—and stimulating—look at "the other Talmud" and the possibilities for Jewish life reflected there.   6 x 9, 256 pp, HC, 978-1-58023-463-4 **$24.99**

**The Torah Revolution:** Fourteen Truths That Changed the World
*By Rabbi Reuven Hammer, PhD*   A unique look at the Torah and the revolutionary teachings of Moses embedded within it that gave birth to Judaism and influenced the world.   6 x 9, 240 pp, HC, 978-1-58023-457-3 **$24.99**

**Ecclesiastes:** Annotated & Explained
*Translation and Annotation by Rabbi Rami Shapiro; Foreword by Rev. Barbara Cawthorne Crafton*
5½ x 8½, 160 pp, Quality PB, 978-1-59473-287-4 **$16.99**

**Ethics of the Sages:** *Pirke Avot—Annotated & Explained   Translation and Annotation by Rabbi Rami Shapiro*   5½ x 8½, 192 pp, Quality PB, 978-1-59473-207-2 **$16.99**

**The Genesis of Leadership:** What the Bible Teaches Us about Vision, Values and Leading Change  *By Rabbi Nathan Laufer; Foreword by Senator Joseph I. Lieberman*
6 x 9, 288 pp, Quality PB, 978-1-58023-352-1 **$18.99**

**Hineini in Our Lives:** Learning How to Respond to Others through 14 Biblical Texts and Personal Stories  *By Rabbi Norman J. Cohen, PhD*  6 x 9, 240 pp, Quality PB, 978-1-58023-274-6 **$16.99**

**A Man's Responsibility:** A Jewish Guide to Being a Son, a Partner in Marriage, a Father and a Community Leader  *By Rabbi Joseph B. Meszler*  6 x 9, 192 pp, Quality PB, 978-1-58023-435-1 **$16.99**

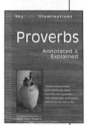

**The Modern Men's Torah Commentary:** New Insights from Jewish Men on the 54 Weekly Torah Portions  *Edited by Rabbi Jeffrey K. Salkin*
6 x 9, 368 pp, HC, 978-1-58023-395-8 **$24.99**

**Moses and the Journey to Leadership:** Timeless Lessons of Effective Management from the Bible and Today's Leaders  *By Rabbi Norman J. Cohen, PhD*
6 x 9, 240 pp, Quality PB, 978-1-58023-351-4 **$18.99**; HC, 978-1-58023-227-2 **$21.99**

**Proverbs:** Annotated & Explained
*Translation and Annotation by Rabbi Rami Shapiro*
5½ x 8½, 288 pp, Quality PB, 978-1-59473-310-9 **$16.99**

**Righteous Gentiles in the Hebrew Bible:** Ancient Role Models for Sacred Relationships
*By Rabbi Jeffrey K. Salkin; Foreword by Rabbi Harold M. Schulweis;*
*Preface by Phyllis Tickle*  6 x 9, 192 pp, Quality PB, 978-1-58023-364-4 **$18.99**

**Sage Tales:** Wisdom and Wonder from the Rabbis of the Talmud
*By Rabbi Burton L. Visotzky*  6 x 9, 256 pp, HC, 978-1-58023-456-6 **$24.99**

**The Wisdom of Judaism:** An Introduction to the Values of the Talmud
*By Rabbi Dov Peretz Elkins*  6 x 9, 192 pp, Quality PB, 978-1-58023-327-9 **$16.99**

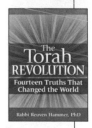

*Or phone, fax, mail or e-mail to:* **JEWISH LIGHTS** Publishing
Sunset Farm Offices, Route 4 • P.O. Box 237 • Woodstock, Vermont 05091
Tel: (802) 457-4000 • Fax: (802) 457-4004 • www.jewishlights.com
*Credit card orders:* **(800) 962-4544** (8:30AM–5:30PM EST Monday–Friday)
Generous discounts on quantity orders. SATISFACTION GUARANTEED. Prices subject to change.

# Social Justice

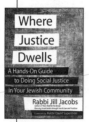

## Where Justice Dwells
A Hands-On Guide to Doing Social Justice in Your Jewish Community
*By Rabbi Jill Jacobs; Foreword by Rabbi David Saperstein*
Provides ways to envision and act on your own ideals of social justice.
7 x 9, 288 pp, Quality PB Original, 978-1-58023-453-5 **$24.99**

## There Shall Be No Needy
Pursuing Social Justice through Jewish Law and Tradition
*By Rabbi Jill Jacobs; Foreword by Rabbi Elliot N. Dorff, PhD; Preface by Simon Greer*
Confronts the most pressing issues of twenty-first-century America from a deeply Jewish perspective. 6 x 9, 288 pp, Quality PB, 978-1-58023-425-2 **$16.99**
**There Shall Be No Needy Teacher's Guide** 8½ x 11, 56 pp, PB, 978-1-58023-429-0 **$8.99**

## Conscience
The Duty to Obey and the Duty to Disobey
*By Rabbi Harold M. Schulweis*
Examines the idea of conscience and the role conscience plays in our relationships to government, law, ethics, religion, human nature, God—and to each other.
6 x 9, 160 pp, Quality PB, 978-1-58023-419-1 **$16.99**; HC, 978-1-58023-375-0 **$19.99**

## Judaism and Justice
The Jewish Passion to Repair the World
*By Rabbi Sidney Schwarz; Foreword by Ruth Messinger*
Explores the relationship between Judaism, social justice and the Jewish identity of American Jews. 6 x 9, 352 pp, Quality PB, 978-1-58023-353-8 **$19.99**

# Spirituality/Women's Interest

## New Jewish Feminism
Probing the Past, Forging the Future
*Edited by Rabbi Elyse Goldstein; Foreword by Anita Diamant*
Looks at the growth and accomplishments of Jewish feminism and what they mean for Jewish women today and tomorrow.
6 x 9, 480 pp, HC, 978-1-58023-359-0 **$24.99**

## The Divine Feminine in Biblical Wisdom Literature
Selections Annotated & Explained
*Translation & Annotation by Rabbi Rami Shapiro*
5½ x 8½, 240 pp, Quality PB, 978-1-59473-109-9 **$16.99**
*(A book from SkyLight Paths, Jewish Lights' sister imprint)*

## The Quotable Jewish Woman
Wisdom, Inspiration & Humor from the Mind & Heart
*Edited by Elaine Bernstein Partnow*
6 x 9, 496 pp, Quality PB, 978-1-58023-236-4 **$19.99**

## The Women's Haftarah Commentary
New Insights from Women Rabbis on the 54 Weekly Haftarah Portions, the 5 Megillot & Special Shabbatot
*Edited by Rabbi Elyse Goldstein*
Illuminates the historical significance of female portrayals in the Haftarah and the Five Megillot. 6 x 9, 560 pp, Quality PB, 978-1-58023-371-2 **$19.99**

## The Women's Torah Commentary
New Insights from Women Rabbis on the 54 Weekly Torah Portions
*Edited by Rabbi Elyse Goldstein*
Over fifty women rabbis offer inspiring insights on the Torah, in a week-by-week format.
6 x 9, 496 pp, Quality PB, 978-1-58023-370-5 **$19.99**; HC, 978-1-58023-076-6 **$34.95**

# Spirituality/Prayer

**Making Prayer Real:** Leading Jewish Spiritual Voices on Why Prayer Is Difficult and What to Do about It  *By Rabbi Mike Comins*
A new and different response to the challenges of Jewish prayer, with "best prayer practices" from Jewish spiritual leaders of all denominations.
6 x 9, 320 pp, Quality PB, 978-1-58023-417-7 **$18.99**

**Witnesses to the One:** The Spiritual History of the *Sh'ma*
*By Rabbi Joseph B. Meszler; Foreword by Rabbi Elyse Goldstein*
6 x 9, 176 pp, Quality PB, 978-1-58023-400-9 **$16.99**; HC, 978-1-58023-309-5 **$19.99**

**My People's Prayer Book Series:** Traditional Prayers, Modern Commentaries  *Edited by Rabbi Lawrence A. Hoffman, PhD*
Provides diverse and exciting commentary to the traditional liturgy. Will help you find new wisdom in Jewish prayer, and bring liturgy into your life. Each book includes Hebrew text, modern translations and commentaries from all perspectives of the Jewish world.

Vol. 1—The *Sh'ma* and Its Blessings
   7 x 10, 168 pp, HC, 978-1-879045-79-8 **$29.99**
Vol. 2—The *Amidah*  7 x 10, 240 pp, HC, 978-1-879045-80-4 **$24.95**
Vol. 3—*P'sukei D'zimrah* (Morning Psalms)
   7 x 10, 240 pp, HC, 978-1-879045-81-1 **$29.99**
Vol. 4—*Seder K'riat Hatorah* (The Torah Service)
   7 x 10, 264 pp, HC, 978-1-879045-82-8 **$29.99**
Vol. 5—*Birkhot Hashachar* (Morning Blessings)
   7 x 10, 240 pp, HC, 978-1-879045-83-5 **$24.95**
Vol. 6—*Tachanun* and Concluding Prayers
   7 x 10, 240 pp, HC, 978-1-879045-84-2 **$24.95**

Vol. 7—Shabbat at Home  7 x 10, 240 pp, HC, 978-1-879045-85-9 **$24.95**
Vol. 8—*Kabbalat Shabbat* (Welcoming Shabbat in the Synagogue)
   7 x 10, 240 pp, HC, 978-1-58023-121-3 **$24.99**
Vol. 9—Welcoming the Night: *Minchah* and *Ma'ariv* (Afternoon and
   Evening Prayer) 7 x 10, 272 pp, HC, 978-1-58023-262-3 **$24.99**
Vol. 10—Shabbat Morning: *Shacharit* and *Musaf* (Morning and
   Additional Services) 7 x 10, 240 pp, HC, 978-1-58023-240-1 **$29.99**

# Spirituality/Lawrence Kushner

**I'm God; You're Not:** Observations on Organized Religion & Other Disguises of the Ego
   6 x 9, 256 pp, Quality PB, 978-1-58023-513-6 **$18.99**; HC, 978-1-58023-441-2 **$21.99**

**The Book of Letters:** A Mystical Hebrew Alphabet
   Popular HC Edition, 6 x 9, 80 pp, 2-color text, 978-1-879045-00-2 **$24.95**
   Collector's Limited Edition, 9 x 12, 80 pp, gold-foil-embossed pages, w/ limited-edition silk-screened print, 978-1-879045-04-0 **$349.00**

**The Book of Miracles:** A Young Person's Guide to Jewish Spiritual Awareness
   6 x 9, 96 pp, 2-color illus., HC, 978-1-879045-78-1 **$16.95** *For ages 9–13*

**The Book of Words:** Talking Spiritual Life, Living Spiritual Talk
   6 x 9, 160 pp, Quality PB, 978-1-58023-020-9 **$18.99**

**Eyes Remade for Wonder:** A Lawrence Kushner Reader  *Introduction by Thomas Moore*
   6 x 9, 240 pp, Quality PB, 978-1-58023-042-1 **$18.95**

**God Was in This Place & I, i Did Not Know:** Finding Self, Spirituality and Ultimate Meaning  6 x 9, 192 pp, Quality PB, 978-1-879045-33-0 **$16.95**

**Honey from the Rock:** An Introduction to Jewish Mysticism
   6 x 9, 176 pp, Quality PB, 978-1-58023-073-5 **$16.95**

**Invisible Lines of Connection:** Sacred Stories of the Ordinary
   5½ x 8½, 160 pp, Quality PB, 978-1-879045-98-9 **$15.95**

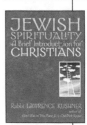

**Jewish Spirituality:** A Brief Introduction for Christians
   5½ x 8½, 112 pp, Quality PB, 978-1-58023-150-3 **$12.95**

**The River of Light:** Jewish Mystical Awareness
   6 x 9, 192 pp, Quality PB, 978-1-58023-096-4 **$16.95**

**The Way Into Jewish Mystical Tradition**
   6 x 9, 224 pp, Quality PB, 978-1-58023-200-5 **$18.99**; HC, 978-1-58023-029-2 **$21.95**

# Inspiration

**God of Me:** Imagining God throughout Your Lifetime
*By Rabbi David Lyon* Helps you cut through preconceived ideas of God and dogmas that stifle your creativity when thinking about your personal relationship with God. 6 x 9, 176 pp, Quality PB, 978-1-58023-452-8 **$16.99**

**The God Upgrade:** Finding Your 21st-Century Spirituality in Judaism's 5,000-Year-Old Tradition *By Rabbi Jamie Korngold; Foreword by Rabbi Harold M. Schulweis* A provocative look at how our changing God concepts have shaped every aspect of Judaism. 6 x 9, 176 pp, Quality PB, 978-1-58023-443-6 **$15.99**

**The Seven Questions You're Asked in Heaven:** Reviewing and Renewing Your Life on Earth *By Dr. Ron Wolfson* An intriguing and entertaining resource for living a life that matters. 6 x 9, 176 pp, Quality PB, 978-1-58023-407-8 **$16.99**

**Happiness and the Human Spirit:** The Spirituality of Becoming the Best You Can Be *By Rabbi Abraham J. Twerski, MD*
Shows you that true happiness is attainable once you stop looking outside yourself for the source. 6 x 9, 176 pp, Quality PB, 978-1-58023-404-7 **$16.99**; HC, 978-1-58023-343-9 **$19.99**

**A Formula for Proper Living:** Practical Lessons from Life and Torah
*By Rabbi Abraham J. Twerski, MD* 6 x 9, 144 pp, HC, 978-1-58023-402-3 **$19.99**

**The Bridge to Forgiveness:** Stories and Prayers for Finding God and Restoring Wholeness *By Rabbi Karyn D. Kedar* 6 x 9, 176 pp, Quality PB, 978-1-58023-451-1 **$16.99**

**The Empty Chair:** Finding Hope and Joy—Timeless Wisdom from a Hasidic Master, Rebbe Nachman of Breslov *Adapted by Moshe Mykoff and the Breslov Research Institute* 4 x 6, 128 pp, Deluxe PB w/ flaps, 978-1-879045-67-5 **$9.99**

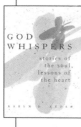

**The Gentle Weapon:** Prayers for Everyday and Not-So-Everyday Moments— Timeless Wisdom from the Teachings of the Hasidic Master, Rebbe Nachman of Breslov *Adapted by Moshe Mykoff and S. C. Mizrahi, together with the Breslov Research Institute* 4 x 6, 144 pp, Deluxe PB w/ flaps, 978-1-58023-022-3 **$9.99**

**God Whispers:** Stories of the Soul, Lessons of the Heart *By Rabbi Karyn D. Kedar* 6 x 9, 176 pp, Quality PB, 978-1-58023-088-9 **$15.95**

**God's To-Do List:** 103 Ways to Be an Angel and Do God's Work on Earth
*By Dr. Ron Wolfson* 6 x 9, 144 pp, Quality PB, 978-1-58023-301-9 **$16.99**

**Jewish Stories from Heaven and Earth:** Inspiring Tales to Nourish the Heart and Soul *Edited by Rabbi Dov Peretz Elkins* 6 x 9, 304 pp, Quality PB, 978-1-58023-363-7 **$16.99**

**Life's Daily Blessings:** Inspiring Reflections on Gratitude and Joy for Every Day, Based on Jewish Wisdom *By Rabbi Kerry M. Olitzky* 4½ x 6½, 368 pp, Quality PB, 978-1-58023-396-5 **$16.99**

**Restful Reflections:** Nighttime Inspiration to Calm the Soul, Based on Jewish Wisdom *By Rabbi Kerry M. Olitzky and Rabbi Lori Forman-Jacobi* 5 x 8, 352 pp, Quality PB, 978-1-58023-091-9 **$16.99**

**Sacred Intentions:** Morning Inspiration to Strengthen the Spirit, Based on Jewish Wisdom *By Rabbi Kerry M. Olitzky and Rabbi Lori Forman-Jacobi* 4½ x 6½, 448 pp, Quality PB, 978-1-58023-061-2 **$16.99**

# Kabbalah/Mysticism

**Jewish Mysticism and the Spiritual Life:** Classical Texts, Contemporary Reflections *Edited by Dr. Lawrence Fine, Dr. Eitan Fishbane and Rabbi Or N. Rose* Inspirational and thought-provoking materials for contemplation, discussion and action. 6 x 9, 256 pp, HC, 978-1-58023-434-4 **$24.99**

**Ehyeh:** A Kabbalah for Tomorrow
*By Rabbi Arthur Green, PhD* 6 x 9, 224 pp, Quality PB, 978-1-58023-213-5 **$18.99**

**The Gift of Kabbalah:** Discovering the Secrets of Heaven, Renewing Your Life on Earth
*By Tamar Frankiel, PhD* 6 x 9, 256 pp, Quality PB, 978-1-58023-141-1 **$16.95**

**Seek My Face:** A Jewish Mystical Theology *By Rabbi Arthur Green, PhD*
6 x 9, 304 pp, Quality PB, 978-1-58023-130-5 **$19.95**

**Zohar:** Annotated & Explained *Translation & Annotation by Dr. Daniel C. Matt; Foreword by Andrew Harvey* 5½ x 8½, 176 pp, Quality PB, 978-1-893361-51-5 **$16.99**
*(A book from SkyLight Paths, Jewish Lights' sister imprint)*

# Spirituality

**The Jewish Lights Spirituality Handbook:** A Guide to Understanding, Exploring & Living a Spiritual Life *Edited by Stuart M. Matlins*
What exactly is "Jewish" about spirituality? How do I make it a part of my life? Fifty of today's foremost spiritual leaders share their ideas and experience with us.
6 x 9, 456 pp, Quality PB, 978-1-58023-093-3 **$19.99**

**The Sabbath Soul:** Mystical Reflections on the Transformative Power of Holy Time *Selection, Translation and Commentary by Eitan Fishbane, PhD*
Explores the writings of mystical masters of Hasidism. Provides translations and interpretations of a wide range of Hasidic sources previously unavailable in English that reflect the spiritual transformation that takes place on the seventh day.
6 x 9, 208 pp, Quality PB, 978-1-58023-459-7 **$18.99**

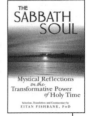

**Repentance:** The Meaning and Practice of *Teshuvah*
*By Dr. Louis E. Newman; Foreword by Rabbi Harold M. Schulweis; Preface by Rabbi Karyn D. Kedar*
Examines both the practical and philosophical dimensions of *teshuvah*, Judaism's core religious-moral teaching on repentance, and its value for us—Jews and non-Jews alike—today. 6 x 9, 256 pp, HC, 978-1-58023-426-9 **$24.99**

**Aleph-Bet Yoga:** Embodying the Hebrew Letters for Physical and Spiritual Well-Being
*By Steven A. Rapp; Foreword by Tamar Frankiel, PhD, and Judy Greenfeld; Preface by Hart Lazer*
7 x 10, 128 pp, b/w photos, Quality PB, Lay-flat binding, 978-1-58023-162-6 **$16.95**

**A Book of Life:** Embracing Judaism as a Spiritual Practice
*By Rabbi Michael Strassfeld* 6 x 9, 544 pp, Quality PB, 978-1-58023-247-0 **$19.99**

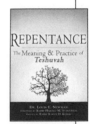

**Bringing the Psalms to Life:** How to Understand and Use the Book of Psalms
*By Rabbi Daniel F. Polish, PhD* 6 x 9, 208 pp, Quality PB, 978-1-58023-157-2 **$16.95**

**Does the Soul Survive?** A Jewish Journey to Belief in Afterlife, Past Lives & Living with Purpose *By Rabbi Elie Kaplan Spitz; Foreword by Brian L. Weiss, MD*
6 x 9, 288 pp, Quality PB, 978-1-58023-165-7 **$16.99**

**Entering the Temple of Dreams:** Jewish Prayers, Movements and Meditations for the End of the Day *By Tamar Frankiel, PhD, and Judy Greenfeld*
7 x 10, 192 pp, illus., Quality PB, 978-1-58023-079-7 **$16.95**

**First Steps to a New Jewish Spirit:** Reb Zalman's Guide to Recapturing the Intimacy & Ecstasy in Your Relationship with God *By Rabbi Zalman M. Schachter-Shalomi with Donald Gropman* 6 x 9, 144 pp, Quality PB, 978-1-58023-182-4 **$16.95**

**Foundations of Sephardic Spirituality:** The Inner Life of Jews of the Ottoman Empire
*By Rabbi Marc D. Angel, PhD* 6 x 9, 224 pp, Quality PB, 978-1-58023-341-5 **$18.99**

**God & the Big Bang:** Discovering Harmony between Science & Spirituality
*By Dr. Daniel C. Matt* 6 x 9, 216 pp, Quality PB, 978-1-879045-89-7 **$18.99**

**God in Our Relationships:** Spirituality between People from the Teachings of Martin Buber *By Rabbi Dennis S. Ross* 5½ x 8½, 160 pp, Quality PB, 978-1-58023-147-3 **$16.95**

**Judaism, Physics and God:** Searching for Sacred Metaphors in a Post-Einstein World
*By Rabbi David W. Nelson* 6 x 9, 352 pp, Quality PB, inc. reader's discussion guide,
978-1-58023-306-4 **$18.99**; HC, 352 pp, 978-1-58023-252-4 **$24.99**

**Meaning & Mitzvah:** Daily Practices for Reclaiming Judaism through Prayer, God, Torah, Hebrew, Mitzvot and Peoplehood *By Rabbi Goldie Milgram*
7 x 9, 336 pp, Quality PB, 978-1-58023-256-2 **$19.99**

**Minding the Temple of the Soul:** Balancing Body, Mind, and Spirit through Traditional Jewish Prayer, Movement, and Meditation *By Tamar Frankiel, PhD, and Judy Greenfeld*
7 x 10, 184 pp, Illus., Quality PB, 978-1-879045-64-4 **$18.99**

**One God Clapping:** The Spiritual Path of a Zen Rabbi *By Rabbi Alan Lew with Sherril Jaffe*
5½ x 8½, 336 pp, Quality PB, 978-1-58023-115-2 **$16.95**

**The Soul of the Story:** Meetings with Remarkable People
*By Rabbi David Zeller* 6 x 9, 288 pp, HC, 978-1-58023-272-2 **$21.99**

**Tanya, the Masterpiece of Hasidic Wisdom:** Selections Annotated & Explained
*Translation & Annotation by Rabbi Rami Shapiro; Foreword by Rabbi Zalman M. Schachter-Shalomi*
5½ x 8½, 240 pp, Quality PB, 978-1-59473-275-1 **$16.99**

**These Are the Words, 2nd Edition:** A Vocabulary of Jewish Spiritual Life
*By Rabbi Arthur Green, PhD* 6 x 9, 320 pp, Quality PB, 978-1-58023-494-8 **$19.99**

# JEWISH LIGHTS BOOKS ARE AVAILABLE FROM BETTER BOOKSTORES. TRY YOUR BOOKSTORE FIRST.

## About Jewish Lights

People of all faiths and backgrounds yearn for books that attract, engage, educate, and spiritually inspire.

Our principal goal is to stimulate thought and help all people learn about who the Jewish People are, where they come from, and what the future can be made to hold. While people of our diverse Jewish heritage are the primary audience, our books speak to people in the Christian world as well and will broaden their understanding of Judaism and the roots of their own faith.

We bring to you authors who are at the forefront of spiritual thought and experience. While each has something different to say, they all say it in a voice that you can hear.

Our books are designed to welcome you and then to engage, stimulate, and inspire. We judge our success not only by whether or not our books are beautiful and commercially successful, but by whether or not they make a difference in your life.

For your information and convenience, at the back of this book we have provided a list of other Jewish Lights books you might find interesting and useful. They cover all the categories of your life:

| | |
|---|---|
| Bar/Bat Mitzvah | Life Cycle |
| Bible Study / Midrash | Meditation |
| Children's Books | Men's Interest |
| Congregation Resources | Parenting |
| Current Events / History | Prayer / Ritual / Sacred Practice |
| Ecology / Environment | Social Justice |
| Fiction: Mystery, Science Fiction | Spirituality |
| Grief / Healing | Theology / Philosophy |
| Holidays / Holy Days | Travel |
| Inspiration | Twelve Steps |
| Kabbalah / Mysticism / Enneagram | Women's Interest |

Stuart M. Matlins, Publisher

*Or phone, fax, mail or e-mail to:* **JEWISH LIGHTS** Publishing
Sunset Farm Offices, Route 4 • P.O. Box 237 • Woodstock, Vermont 05091
Tel: (802) 457-4000 • Fax: (802) 457-4004 • www.jewishlights.com
***Credit card orders:*** **(800) 962-4544** (8:30AM–5:30PM EST Monday–Friday)
*Generous discounts on quantity orders. SATISFACTION GUARANTEED. Prices subject to change.*

**For more information about each book, visit our website at www.jewishlights.com**